Longman exam
practice kit

A-Level
Psychology

Alison Wadeley

LONGMAN

Series Editors
Geoff Black and Stuart Wall

Titles available

A-level
Biology
Business Studies
Chemistry
Mathematics
Psychology
Sociology

Addison Wesley Longman Ltd.,
Edinburgh Gate, Harlow,
Essex CM20 2JE, England
and Associated Companies throughout the World.

First Published 1997

ISBN 0582-30390-7

British Library Cataloguing-in-Publication Data
A catalogue record for this book is available from the British Library.

Set by 8 in 11/13pt Baskerville
Printed by Longman Asia Limited, Hong Kong

ACKNOWLEDGEMENTS

I should like to thank my long-time colleague and friend Mike (the 'Animal in
Psychology') Cardwell for his invaluable advice during the preparation of this
book and for altruism that is not apparent but real.

This book is dedicated with love to Ian, Holly and Imogen whose tolerance
and support is so very much appreciated.

The author is grateful to the following examination boards for permission to
use their questions:

► The Associated Examining Board (AEB)
► The Northern Examinations and Assessment Board (NEAB).

These boards accept no responsibility for the accuracy of the answers
provided. They are the responsibility of the author alone.

Contents

How to use this book

This book seeks to help you achieve a good grade in your A- or AS-level psychology examination. It covers core topics which are common to all exam boards and some other topics that are very likely to be on your syllabus.

The book is arranged in four parts:

Part I   Preparing for the examination

Here we consider some useful techniques you might use before and during the examination. A Revision Planner is provided to help you structure your run-up to the exam. The different *types* of question you will face are considered, along with tips to help you answer them successfully. It is vital that you correctly interpret the questions that are set, so I carefully define, in a glossary, some of the key words you are likely to find in questions, such as **define**, **assess**, **justify**, and the skills the examiner is looking for.

Part II   Topic areas, summaries and questions

Here, I identify nine key topic areas which are especially relevant to the AEB syllabus but which also cover substantial areas of the NEAB and OCSEB syllabuses. For *each* of these you will find the following:

1 **Revision tips,** giving specific guidance on revising that particular topic area;
2 **Topic outlines,** briefly summarizing the key points of theory/research/ practice in that topic area;
3 **Revision activities,** to help make your revision active, exercises which will help you self-check your understanding of that topic area; and
4 **Practice questions,** questions of the type you are likely to encounter in your exam.

It is essential that you try the questions yourself before checking with the answers provided to all activities and questions in Part III of the book.

Part III   Answers and grading

Here you will find answers to the activities and practice questions set for each topic area. The answers to essay questions are actual student answers with examiner comments to identify the strengths and weaknesses along with a suggested mark. Skill A material has been differentiated from Skill B material: Skill A is presented in ordinary type, while Skill B appears in italic, see page 2.

Part IV   Timed practice papers with answers

Here you will find sample papers or parts of papers to give you practice in timing yourself under exam-type conditions *before* the exam. Examiner's comments and outline answers are provided to these questions so that you can check your performance.

part I

Preparing for the examination

Planning your revision

▶ Start revising in good time. Advance planning really helps. Last-minute revision does work for some people but, on the whole, it is too risky.

▶ Identify and list topics which make up the compulsory 'core' of your syllabus. You will be required to answer at least some questions on these. Chapters 7, 8 and 9 in this book are vital for all students as they cover core topics which underpin your whole syllabus.

▶ Complete your list by adding enough topics from the specialist areas you have covered to ensure that you will be able to answer the required number of questions. You will now have identified your 'bottom line' revision. Use the syllabus to help you here. Once you have covered the bare minimum, add as much as you can to it to improve your chances in the examination.

▶ Plan your revision carefully. Make a Revision Planner to ensure you can fit in what you need to do. A timetable you can use for this purpose is included in this book. Fill in your weekly revision using the 'Tips' listed on the planner.

▶ Try to allocate set times each week when you are going to revise a particular subject. Make sure you have enough 'slots' to cover everything you will need.

▶ Make a plan that works for *you*. Everyone works best in their own way. But remember, even though you may work best in the middle of the night, exams happen in the day, so make sure you are accustomed to working between the daytime hours when exams are likely to be scheduled.

▶ Be prepared to adapt your timetable as you go along. Some topics will take more or less time than you imagined. Build in rest periods for relaxation and treats. These will help to keep you going. If you are working hard, you deserve them so take them without feeling guilty.

▶ Revise actively. This means doing more than just reading over something. You may fool yourself into thinking you have learned a topic simply because you understand it and recognize the ideas when you read over them. This is not the same as being able to reproduce those ideas in an exam. At the very least, you should re-work your notes into as many different forms as you can, e.g. make 'brain maps' of the kind shown on page 11, or lists of key points on postcards. Discuss the topics with your teacher and friends, in or out of class.

▶ Practise reproducing information without the help of notes or books, for example by completing the revision activities and examination questions. Try to have a practice run of the exam before the real thing. Recite model answers to yourself while you are lying in the bath. Risk social ridicule by talking to the dog about Pavlov's conditioning experiments every time you take it for a walk. Worry your parents with accounts of child-rearing styles and their effects. Alienate your fellow students by telling them about the unreliability of memory – and then win them back by telling them how they can improve it.

▶ Expect to work hard. Sadly, few of us are natural geniuses who soak up information with little effort. You will need to put in the hours, but remember the *quality* of your revision is more important than the *quantity*.

▶ Look after yourself. Eat, sleep and rest well. Socialize, exercise and learn to manage your feelings of stress. The person (i.e. you) who is going to write all those examination answers must be in good shape.

Using examination questions in revision

After you have revised a topic area it is vital that you carefully consider examination questions of the type you will face in the exam. Attempt the sample question at the end of each chapter in Part II of this book yourself, before looking at the answers in Part III. This will help you to:

► check that you have really understood the topic you have been revising;
► reveal any gaps in your knowledge. It is certainly best to discover what these are *before* the exam when there is still time to put things right;
► identify the sort of questions you do well and, perhaps, some to avoid!
► become familiar with the type of language used in examination questions. See also the list of 'command words' used by examiners on the following page;
► check your answers against the marked student answers and the outline answers provided;
► fine-tune your timing.

Once you feel that your preparation is complete, set yourself a mock exam using the practice papers in Part IV. You might like to start with just one 45-minute answer and build up to more as you become more experienced. If you are an A-level student sitting terminal exams, you will need to be able to plan and write answers for up to three hours. Students following modular routes may sit shorter examinations. Check your own syllabus.

Types of examination question

This will depend on which syllabus you are following. The AEB asks mainly essay questions, sometimes breaking these down into smaller parts. The NEAB and OCSEB use a variety of formats, some requiring very short answers and some providing stimulus material to set the scene for questions. All exam boards test knowledge of research methodology and statistics. To do this the AEB and NEAB use stimulus material and a series of short questions. The OCSEB sets candidates an assignment in which they have to devise and report a way of testing a given research question. Generally, AEB style questions of the kind likely to appear on the new syllabus 1997 question papers and beyond are used in this book. Past papers can be purchased from exam boards.

Assessment objectives in psychology

In the AEB examination, the examiner's objective is to assess your ability in four skill domains. These are very similar, whichever board's syllabus you are following. Skills A, B and D count for 80% of your grade. They are:

► **Skill A**　This includes knowledge, description and understanding of appropriate theories, concepts, evidence and applications. Your answer should also be well organized so as to give a coherent answer to the question.
► **Skill B**　This includes well-balanced and well-argued analysis and evaluation – and, where relevant, interpretation – of relevant theories, concepts, evidence and applications.
► **Skill C**　Research skills are assessed in coursework.
► **Skill D**　Quality of language. You must demonstrate that you can express ideas clearly and accurately and that you are competent in the use of grammar, punctuation, spelling and the use of specialist terminology. This skill accounts for 5% of your total mark, with 1% of this being assessed in coursework.

Command words used in questions

Listed here are the AEB's glossary of terms, injunctions or commands that examiners use in questions to encourage you to demonstrate your skills.

Skill A terms

▶ **Consider** Requires the candidate to demonstrate knowledge and understanding of the stipulated topic area.

▶ **Define** Requires the candidate to explain what is meant by a particular term such as one used to identify a particular concept.

▶ **Describe** Requires the candidate to present evidence of their knowledge of the stipulated topic area.

▶ **Examine** Requires the candidate to present a detailed, descriptive consideration of the stipulated topic area.

▶ **Outline/state** Requires the candidate to offer a summary description of the stipulated topic area in brief form.

Skill B terms

▶ **Analyse/critically analyse** Requires the candidate to demonstrate understanding through consideration of the components or elements of the stipulated topic area.

▶ **Assess/critically assess** Requires the candidate to make an informed judgement about how good or effective something is, based on an awareness of the strengths and limitations of the information and argument presented. The candidate is required to present a considered appraisal of the topic areas.

▶ **Criticize** Requires the candidate to critically appraise/evaluate the strengths/weaknesses of the stipulated topic areas.

▶ **Evaluate/critically evaluate** Requires the candidate to make an informed judgement about the value of the stipulated topic areas, based on systematic analysis and examination.

▶ **Justify** Requires the candidate to consider the grounds for a decision, by offering a supportive consideration of the logic behind a particular interpretation.

Skill A and B terms

▶ **Compare/contrast** Requires the candidate to consider similarities and/or differences between the stipulated topic area (e.g. psychological theories or concepts). This may involve critical consideration of points of similarity and differentiation.

▶ **Critically consider** As 'consider' (above), but the candidate is also required to indicate the strengths and limitations of the material presented.

▶ **Distinguish between** Requires the candidate to demonstrate their understanding of the differences between two stipulated topic areas (e.g. theories). Such a differentiation might be achieved at the levels of both descriptive and critical contrasting.

▶ **Discuss** Requires the candidate both to describe and evaluate by reference to different if not contrasting points of view. This may be done sequentially or concurrently. Questions may instruct the candidate to discuss with reference to particular criteria, for example, by the use of the phrase 'in terms of'.

How marks are allocated

AEB essay questions each carry 24 marks. A general mark scheme is outlined for you here. With every question, examiners are also given specific information to help them mark particular questions. In split questions, marks may be divided e.g. 12/12 in which case the 24-mark mark scheme is divided up and marks awarded pro-rata to the various parts of the answer.

Table 1: A general mark scheme for AEB A- and AS-level essay questions

Band	Marks	Skill A (description, knowledge and understanding)	Skill B (analysis, evaluation and interpretation)
		Marking criteria	Marking criteria
Band 1	0–4	Bottom: Weak, muddled, incomplete. May be largely irrelevant. Top: Basic, rudimentary, sometimes flawed, sometimes focused on the question.	Bottom: Weak, muddled, incomplete. May be largely irrelevant. Top: Basic, rudimentary, sometimes flawed. Restricted, minimal interpretation.
Band 2	5–8	Bottom: Limited and lacking detail. Some evidence of organization, breadth and depth. Top: Reasonably accurate and detailed. Increasing evidence of organization, breadth and depth.	Bottom: Relevant but limited, reasonably effective, some elaboration. Top: Relevant but slightly limited, effective with coherent elaboration.
Band 3	9–12	Bottom: Slightly limited, but generally well-detailed. Coherent organization. Evidence of breadth and depth although these may not be well-balanced. Top: Accurate, well-detailed, coherent organization. Substantial breadth and depth and a good balance between these.	Bottom: Informed, effective, appropriate and coherently elaborated. Top: Informed, highly effective, thorough and coherently elaborated.

During the examination

▶ Think positive. All that hard revision is over. Now you can only do your best.

▶ Relax. Well – relax as much as you can. A little bit of tension is a good thing because it energizes you but too much anxiety can spoil things.

▶ Ignore what others are doing around you, especially the annoying person who asks for extra paper before you've finished your first page.

▶ Read the instructions at the start of the paper.

▶ Follow the instructions. You would be surprised how many students don't.

▶ Read through all the questions that are relevant to you at least once.

▶ Take time to think about each question, paying attention to the wording and the number of marks to be gained. The questions you choose should be those that will earn you the most marks. They may not be on your favourite topics.

▶ Plan your time carefully and try to stick to your plan.

▶ Answer the question that is set and not the one you wish had been set. A good check that you have done this is to ask yourself if someone else could work out what the question was just from reading your answer. If they could, you have probably done a good job.

▶ Build as much psychology into your answer as you can. Use theories and research evidence whenever possible to back up your ideas.

▶ Try to evaluate the theories and evidence in answers to questions that invite evaluation. Remember that in the AEB exam, Skills A and B are equally weighted so you must show evidence of both to the very best of your ability.

part II
Topic areas, summaries and questions

Social psychology

This chapter concentrates on an area of social psychology known as social influence and chooses key topics to illustrate this diverse area. In general, social influence covers any situation in which people have an effect on each other's judgements, opinions, attitudes or behaviour. Such influence may result from the presence of anything from one to many people and, sometimes, other people do not even need to be physically present to influence us.

There are some old favourites on A-level syllabuses for this area of psychology. Try not to get too involved in the detail of the classic studies. There are important things to be learned from them but new developments are just as important, so bring in more up-to-date material as much as you can.

TOPIC OUTLINES

Conformity, obedience and independent behaviour

Conformity

- ▶ Aronson (1992) defines conformity as a change in a person's behaviour as a result of real or imagined pressure from a person or group of people. Lay people think of conformity as giving in to group pressure. Mann (1969) offers a classification which includes normative conformity (i.e. compliance and true conformity) informational conformity and ingratiational conformity.
- ▶ There are two types of non-conformity: independent behaviour and anti-conformity. In the latter, a person always goes against the group, usually out of perverseness.
- ▶ Classic studies include those by Sherif (1935) on the autokinetic effect and the formation of group norms, Asch (1956) on group pressure and Crutchfield (1954) who modified and extended Asch's work. Asch and Crutchfield discovered many variables which affected the rate of conformity in their studies. In particular, Asch varied task difficulty, group size, the presence of allies, the status of other group members and the conditions of responding. Crutchfield varied the type of problem people had to respond to. Both found wide variation in people's tendency to conform.
- ▶ Moscovici (1976) questioned whether majority influence alone was enough to explain such results. He showed a minority could also be influential providing it held consistently to its view.
- ▶ Perrin and Spencer (1981) thought that the Asch effect could be 'a child of its time' reflecting the historical and cultural state of 1950s USA. In fact, results in other studies do seem to vary across time and culture.
- ▶ Kelman (1958) has suggested three more reasons why people conform: compliance, identification and internalization. Post-experimental interviews suggested Asch's participants had complied compared to Sherif's participants who seemed to have internalized the group view.
- ▶ Behavioural contagion explains how social behaviour patterns can be catching. People may conform almost without thought because of this influence.

▶ Deindividuation is another possible reason for conformity, as shown in Zimbardo's (1973) prison-simulation study.

▶ Ethical considerations are raised by studies such as these, particularly with respect to deception and causing people psychological discomfort.

Obedience

▶ Obedience is when a person behaves in a particular way because they have been told to do so by someone else (perhaps an authority figure). Some psychologists define it as an extreme form of compliance.

▶ In Milgram's (1963) classic study of obedience to an experimenter, 62.5% of 40 adult male volunteers were prepared to deliver increasingly powerful electric shocks to another person, allegedly in the course of teaching them something.

▶ Variations of the study included choosing a less impressive venue, bringing the participant closer to their victim, adding stooges who behaved in various ways (e.g. withdrawing half way through), varying the proximity of the experimenter and testing women (who showed similar obedience rates to men).

▶ Obedience studies raise important ethical issues. Baumrind (1964) criticized Milgram's research procedures but he successfully defended himself. In fact although he was temporarily suspended he was later exonerated and the research design was judged to be within the realms of acceptability.

▶ It is difficult to compare cross-cultural attempts to replicate Milgram's studies because they often use different kinds of participants or 'learners'. However, in a study in Australia, Kilham and Mann (1974) found 40% of male and 16% of female students were obedient. In Spain, Miranda *et al.* (1981) found over 90% obedience in students. Other findings vary between these two extremes.

▶ Zimbardo's prison-simulation study showed that, even in role play, individuals will subjugate themselves to the power of others.

▶ Real-life settings involve complex relationships between the authority and the obedient person. Hofling (1966) tested 22 nurses on duty on private psychiatric hospital wards. Twenty-one of them obeyed a telephoned instruction from a doctor they did not know to give an unfamiliar drug to a patient. This was almost 100% obedience.

▶ Milgram's agency theory was developed to explain his own findings. He suggested human social behaviour is essentially hierarchical and we will sometimes subjugate ourselves and become the agents of authority or, in other situations, act autonomously. Such a view places unjustified responsibility on the individual rather than the wider social situation.

▶ Individual differences in attitudes to obedience have been shown to vary with religious commitment, educational level and socioeconomic status.

▶ Staub (1990) considers that bystanders who are passive and who tolerate authority contribute as much to the effect as the authority itself, for example, in allowing wartime atrocities to take place.

Independent behaviour

▶ Independent behaviour is about resisting any kind of social influence. Understanding independence is linked to research into conformity, obedience and the influence of audiences, leaders, bystanders, advertisers or propagandists.

▶ In Asch's experiments, independent behaviour was far more common than conformity. Two reasons are suggested: a desire to:

1 maintain uniqueness and individuality even if this puts one's acceptance in the group at risk; and

2 maintain a sense of control over events. Burger (1987) measured participants' desire for personal control and found high scorers resisted conformity in rating the funniness of jokes.

▶ On resisting obedience, Baron and Byrne (1991) say if individuals in experiments are encouraged to remind themselves that they, not the authority, will be actually committing the deed, obedience drops.

▶ Exposure to disobedient models is often effective in encouraging independence. For example, stooges who 'dropped out' of Milgram's experiment increased the drop-out rate in 'teacher' participants.

▶ Encouraging people to question the expertise and motives of authorities is helpful. Are they really expert? What do they have to gain?

▶ Informing people about research findings such as Milgram's could help to inoculate them against attempts to get them to obey.

▶ Tendency to act independently may be linked to level of moral reasoning (Kohlberg, 1969).

▶ Cultural values and independence may be linked. Cross-cultural replications of Milgram's obedience experiments yield mixed results.

▶ Resisting authority can be dangerous but there may be a choice. Courageous leaders can act as disobedient models against oppressive regimes. Baron and Byrne (1991) say 'Tyrants cannot remain in power when large numbers of citizens refuse to obey.'

Social power, leadership and followership

▶ Social power refers to the ability of one or more people to bring about behaviour change in others.

▶ It is a feature of many forms of social influence, e.g. in conformity and obedience.

▶ It can be expressed non-verbally as a way of regulating social relationships, for example, in the workplace bosses (or workers) can signal power (or subordination) by the way they use eye contact, personal space and touching.

▶ Power can be manipulated in many types of relationship through techniques of self-presentation, such as ingratiation, intimidation, self-promotion, exemplification or supplication.

▶ Power is particularly closely linked with leadership and followership. French and Raven (1960) offer five kinds of leadership power:
1 legitimate power: formal power carried by a role e.g. teacher, President;
2 reward power: possessed by someone who has control over valued resources;
3 coercive power: used by someone who can control unpleasant consequences for their followers;
4 expert power: possessed by someone with special knowledge or expertise;
5 referent power: possessed by someone with particular personal qualities such as charisma.

▶ 'Leaders are members of groups who are particularly influential and who act to guide, direct and motivate the group to achieve its goals' (Hollander, 1985).

▶ Trait theories or 'great man/woman' theories hold the view that 'leaders are born, not made', that is, they have certain personal attributes. Compared to non-leaders, there is evidence that leaders:
  – have slightly higher than average intelligence;
  – tend to be more sociable, energetic and out-going;
  – have higher than average needs for achievement and affiliation;
  – are taller; and
  – may express their traits in a particular style – task-oriented, socioemotional (relationship oriented), democratic, *laissez-faire* or authoritarian.

▶ Leadership style may affect how much power can be wielded. Lewin *et al.* (1939) arranged for ten-year-old boys to experience democratic, authoritarian or *laissez-faire* styles. Boys in the first group were happier and more productive than in either of the other two.

▶ Situational theories emphasize the role of context in the emergence of leaders and give examples such as Churchill and Hitler in the Second World War.

Leaders may emerge if their skills are relevant in a certain situation or because of their central position in a communication network.

▶ Interactional or contingency theories stress both traits and situations e.g. Fiedler (1978) talked of task-oriented and socioemotional types performing better in different situations. (His Least Preferred Co-worker (LPC) measure can be used to identify leader type.) He suggested task-oriented leaders are better in situations of high or low favourability and socioemotional leaders would be better in situations of medium favourability. However:
  – Nebeker (1977) found that leaders could switch between the two types if circumstances demanded it. Indeed, Blake and Mouton (1982) found that the most effective leaders were good at both types;
  – leaders' behaviour is not always as consistent as this theory suggests;
  – there may be more than one leader, e.g. one formal and one or more informal;
  – followers may select the leader according to the type of task they are facing.

▶ Leadership expectation may affect power. McGregor (1960) talked of Theory X managers who regard workers as inherently lazy and Theory Y managers who see workers as needing and enjoying work. There is some weak evidence that the manager's attitude could become a self-fulfilling prophecy and affect how much workers are prepared to do.

▶ House (1971) proposed the path–goal theory of leadership: good leaders make their expectations clear but also allow people to satisfy their own goals.

▶ More recent models emphasize, as Fiedler did, the two-way process between leaders and followers:
  – transactional leaders concentrate on the quality of the interactions they have with their subordinates. Followers feel their views are taken into account more and consequently seem to notice overall leadership style less;
  – transformational leaders are needed to bring about change. They are good at managing a group's values and giving it a sense of identity and vision. They come to 'stand for' the group (Smith and Peterson, 1988). Bob Geldof's leadership of Live Aid is a good example.

Collective behaviour

This is a wide term that covers many aspects of behaviour. Here, it is taken to denote situations in which individuals behave in similar ways or experience similar things because they are together – the group is 'greater than the sum of its parts'. In this section we will use crowd and mob behaviour as examples of collective behaviour.

▶ Types of crowd: include political, religious, sporting, social and casual (e.g. shoppers). Brown (1965) identified acquisitive, escaping, expressive and aggressive crowds.

▶ There are many social influences in crowds: deindividuation, group polarisation, social facilitation, frustration, bystander apathy, behavioural contagion, social comparison, learned helplessness and feeling psychologically crowded.

▶ Early theories:
  1 LeBon (1895) talked of 'group mind' and perpetuated the idea of primitive mobs. This helped to legitimize middle-class reactions to the collective expression of political disenchantment in the working classes, such as marches, demonstrations and strikes.
  2 Allport (1924) said the individual in a crowd is still an individual, 'only more so'. Certain personality types become exaggerated in different crowd situations.

▶ Zimbardo's deindividuation theory is like a modern version of LeBon's. The basic idea, supported by research, is that anonymity releases the usual restraints on behaviour. The effects of this can be both positive and negative.

- Reicher (1982) criticized Zimbardo's approach for being reductionist, arguing that collective behaviour is more than the sum of anonymous individuals' behaviour. He said crowd behaviour is rarely haphazard. Instead it is sophisticated and has clear limits, both geographically and in terms of what people do. He uses the example of the St Paul's riots in Bristol in 1980.
- Borrowing from Tajfel's (1981) social identity theory, Reicher suggests a crowd is a social group with a common identity. This gives rise to homogenous (similar) behaviour between members. It explains why they behave as they do (according to perceived group norms) and why activities are limited geographically (e.g. football fans' 'patch').
- Waddington *et al.* (1987) said most explanations are too simple. Incidents need to be examined on six levels: (1) structural (the wider social situation, such as level of unemployment); (2) political and ideological; (3) cultural; (4) contextual (such as the timing of the incident); (5) situational (the venue); and (6) interactional (between the people involved).
- In a comparison of one peaceful and one violent incident in the 1984 miners' strike, differences were found on contextual, situational and interactional levels but other levels were similar.
- Football supporters often have clear rules and rituals of aggression. If authorities upset these, the situation between rivals may be aggravated.
- Political crowds are often said to erupt because of 'flashpoints' but this is too simplistic.
- Can these theories inform 'crowd managers'? Waddington *et al.* suggest tackling crowd behaviour on as many of the six levels as possible: let the crowd police itself, liaison between organizers and police, use of minimum force by police, ensure police are accountable to the community, train crowd managers in interpersonal skills.

REVISION ACTIVITY • CROWD AND MOB BEHAVIOUR

This activity traces the development of theories of crowd behaviour and offers some ideas about how to manage crowds. On page 11 you will find a partially completed brain map on crowd behaviour. Try to do as much of it as you can from Topic Outline 3. The completed brain map on page 66 will help you to fill in any gaps. Your aim should be to remember the entire brain map, so once you feel confident, reproduce the whole thing on a blank sheet of paper.

A certain amount of prior knowledge is assumed here. If you know nothing about this area, two helpful sources are:

- Banyard, P. and Hayes, N. (1994) *Psychology: Theory and Application*, London: Chapman & Hall.
- Hayes, N. (1994) *Foundations of Psychology*, London: Routledge.

ESSAY QUESTION

Critically consider psychological explanations of social power in relation to leadership. *(24 marks)*

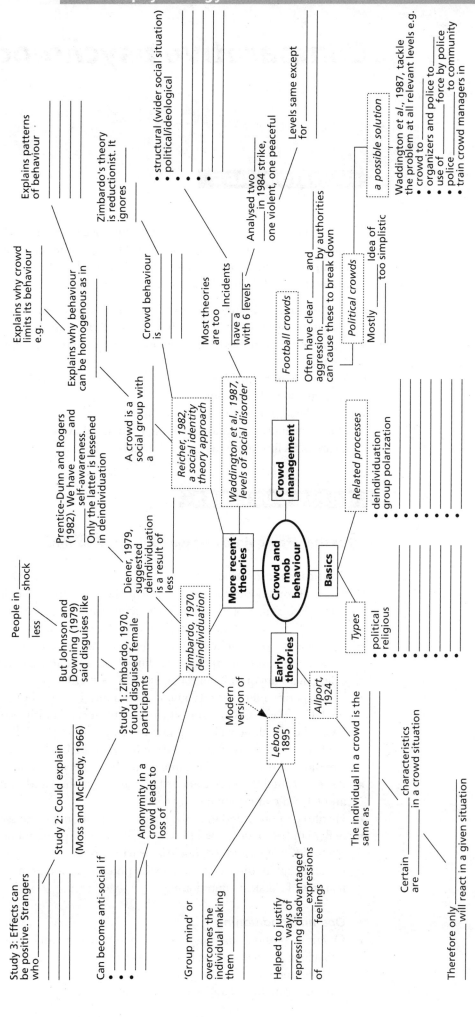

Figure 1: Crowd and mob behaviour: partially completed brain map.

2 Comparative psychology

This section examines some of the ways in which our understanding of behaviour can be enhanced by comparing species and considering the influence of evolutionary and biological factors. The topics used to illustrate this approach include learning, animal language and evolutionary explanations of human behaviour.

▶ On 'learning' it is important to cover more than laboratory studies of conditioning so that you know how such explanations have been challenged.
▶ Know some examples of learning in the natural environment (e.g. foraging and homing).
▶ Your study of animal language should ideally cover examples of natural animal language as well as attempts to teach language to animals.
▶ An understanding of the evolutionary approach will give you a good overview of its contribution to understanding human behaviour, but you should also be aware of its limitations as an explanation.

TOPIC OUTLINES

Classical (Pavlovian) and operant conditioning

Classical conditioning
▶ Classical conditioning is a type of learning which can explain how we develop fears, phobias and other emotional reactions and food aversions. Ivan Pavlov (1849–1936), was the first to study it formally, using the dog's digestive processes.
▶ First of all there must be an innate reflex action: an automatic, involuntary response to a stimulus such as startling in response to a sudden stimulus. Pavlov called these unconditional reflexes (UCS → UCR).
▶ The experimenter presents a neutral stimulus (NS) just before or along with the UCS. The UCR occurs as before. After several pairings of the NS and UCS, the NS alone will be enough to bring about the UCR at which point the NS becomes a CS (conditional stimulus) and the UCR becomes a CR (conditional response). The animal now has a new conditional reflex.
▶ Pavlov stressed the importance of contiguity (timing) and similarity of the NS and UCS if conditioning is to occur.
▶ He also demonstrated that higher-order conditioning is possible.
▶ Seligman (1970) described the 'Sauce Bearnaise' phenomenon – an example of classically conditioned, one trial learning.
▶ Generalization, discrimination, extinction and spontaneous recovery are all features of classical conditioning.

Operant conditioning
▶ Operant conditioning is used to describe how sometimes complicated behaviour patterns can be built up over time, such as skill acquisition in humans and maze-learning in rats. Behaviour patterns can be altered and refined through trial and error, and built up by shaping.

▶ There does not need to be an innate reflex to begin with. The animal's behaviour is not respondent but voluntary: it 'operates' on its environment to produce an effect, hence the name 'operant'.

▶ Research into operant conditioning is said to have started with Edward Thorndike's (1874–1949) 'instrumental conditioning'. His 'cats in a puzzle box' studies led him to formulate his Law of Effect which states that if a response is followed by a satisfying state of affairs it tends to be repeated. Inconsequential responses fade away.

▶ B. F. Skinner (1904–1990) developed the theory of instrumental conditioning into a theory of operant conditioning using rats or pigeons in Skinner boxes. Skinner concluded that behaviour was determined by its consequences and could be shaped and maintained by its consequences (reinforcements and punishments).

▶ Reinforcement can be primary or secondary. Scheduled (occasional or partial) reinforcement leads to behaviour that is more resistant to extinction.

▶ Generalization, discrimination and extinction are all features of operant conditioning.

Challenges to traditional learning theory

The cognitive challenge: this emphasizes that mental processes/cognitions cannot be disregarded

▶ Cognitive theories of learning include Tolman's theory of latent learning, Kohler's (1925) work on insight learning and Harlow's (1939) work on learning sets and transfer of learning. There is also evidence of cultural transmission/observational learning in animal behaviour. All these demonstrate the importance of cognitive factors in non-human animal and human learning.

▶ Other theorists say that animals are capable of developing expectancies, for example, that a UCS will follow a CS (Bindra, 1968) or that a particular outcome will follow a response (Bolles, 1979). Expectancies have survival value and can account for conditioning phenomena and flexibility in responses. Expectancies may be innate, learned or both. Therefore this links to:

The biological challenge: this emphasizes different learning capacities within and between species

▶ The 'Garcia effect' refers to how we can be biologically unprepared, prepared or contra-prepared to make certain associations. The 'Sauce Bearnaise' phenomenon (Seligman, 1970) is an example of our preparedness to associate sickness with certain foods via classical conditioning.

▶ Breland and Breland (1961) talked of 'instinctive drift' after finding that animals such as pigs and racoons cannot be operantly conditioned to learn certain tricks as their behaviour tends to revert to instinctive patterns.

REVISION ACTIVITY • BRAINSTORMING CONDITIONING THEORIES

Provide answers to the following questions. Then check what you have done against the answers suggested on pages 67–68.

1 What sorts of behaviour does classical conditioning explain best?
2 Define the term 'reflex'.
3 Draw diagrams to show how classical conditioning could account for:
   ▶ a child's fear of men in white coats; and
   ▶ an adult's aversion to lemon meringue pie.

4 To what might a classically conditioned fear of budgerigars generalize?
5 How might you train a dog to discriminate between rectangles and squares?
6 What kinds of learned behaviour does operant conditioning explain?
7 How would you use shaping to teach a rat to pick up a marble and drop it into a cup?
8 Distinguish between negative reinforcement and punishment.
9 Define the term 'extinction'.
10 Give one example each of latent learning, insight and learning set.
11 Explain the role of expectancies in conditioning theories.
12 Explain the terms 'instinctive drift' and briefly say why it challenges traditional conditioning theory.

Learning in the natural environment: foraging and homing behaviour

Foraging

In order to survive, animals must search for food, discriminate it from inedible items and then catch it. Food may be static or move around and will be differently distributed. Finding it therefore involves various search techniques, some of which are very flexible. The exact form this behaviour takes is influenced by body size, diet, digestive system, current physiological state and the presence of young and inherited behaviour patterns. But learning can also play an important part. The influence of learning varies between species:

▶ Little learning seems to be involved in a toad's tendency to snap at small, dark, moving objects.

▶ In chicks, 'prey' recognition takes practice, i.e. they have to form a 'search image'.

▶ Rats sample small amounts of many potential foods. If sickness follows any one food they learn to avoid it and anything resembling it (classically conditioned one-trial learning).

▶ Stalking techniques in solitary or cooperative hunters are very flexible and can change as the situation develops. Certain tactics are more likely to be repeated if they pay off (operant conditioning: shaping and partial reinforcement schedules).

▶ Rhesus monkey juveniles on Cayo, Santiago, learn to wash food by observing what adults do.

Optimal foraging theory (OFT) is based on the assumption that foraging uses up energy and/or can expose the animal to risk from predators, so the benefits must outweigh the costs if the animal is to survive and reproduce. OFT is supported by many aspects of foraging behaviour:

▶ Optimizing diet. Certain species of crow feed on whelks by dropping them on to rocks to break the shell. Larger whelks are heavier to carry than smaller ones but are more likely to break on impact, so there is a net saving in energy and proportionally more nourishment. Some species of animal switch prey quite suddenly. It has been speculated that this is for nutritional reasons.

▶ Optimizing choice of search patch and time expended. Bumble bees forage in the most profitable places and move on when gain becomes marginal. Larger birds, such as osprey, hover less than smaller ones, such as hummingbirds, for whom hovering is more energy efficient. Chipmunks fill their pouches with more food the further they are from 'home'.

▶ Optimizing search paths. Toads tend to lie in wait. Thrushes can adjust the angle and length of their jumps according to whether food is clumped or scattered. Lionesses hunt by stealth and often cooperatively. In general, animals move in patterns that maximize the chances of obtaining food.

The role of learning in OFT is not clearly defined. Foraging patterns may be innate or learned or both. In the latter case, animals may inherit a preference for a particular behaviour pattern but also be able to use it flexibly for greater gain. This flexibility should give a selective advantage to certain individuals. They would be more likely to survive and reproduce, and their young would inherit their parents' adaptive flexibility.

Homing

A sense of direction is a useful adaptive characteristic for many species of animal. It is well known that salmon 'home' to their natal river for breeding and that they depend on stream odour to do so. Certain species of bird and mammal can migrate over long distances and many animals simply need to be able to navigate so that they can find food or return to young or safety. The ability of pigeons to 'home' has led to much speculation about the mechanisms behind homing:

► Navigation by the sun. Kramer (1953) proposed the map–compass hypothesis, saying that pigeons take a compass-bearing from the sun and then use some sort of internal map to navigate. To do this, the pigeon would also need an internal clock. Indeed, experiments shifting the timing of pigeons' internal clocks do lead to navigational errors of the kind predicted by this theory but the nature of the proposed internal map and compass remain unclear.

► Navigation by magnetic sense. Walcott *et al.* (1979) showed that pigeons have a structure between the skull and the brain which contains 'magnetite' and which could be part of an internal compass. Interference with its magnetism affects pigeon's homing ability, but only on overcast days when they cannot use the sun.

► Navigation by cognitive map. Pigeons may have internal 'maps'. If so, what is their form and how are they learned? Pigeons who are anaesthetized on the outward journey or who wear translucent goggles can still 'home' so it is not simply a question of learning the outward route and reversing it.

► Navigation by infrasound. This is sound too low for humans to hear. It travels slowly and for very long distances and is emitted by geological features such as mountain ranges. Blakemore (1984) suggested this could provide special kinds of landmark or 'signpost' to help in navigation.

► Navigation by olfaction. This is a less likely explanation of pigeon-homing, as their sense of smell is not particularly acute. It is also difficult to test since plugging their nostrils or otherwise interfering with olfaction tends to upset their general behaviour.

The exact mechanisms of homing in pigeons remain a mystery. There may be a hierarchy of preferred senses since, from a survival point of view, over-dependence on one alone would be very risky. Homing ability probably results from a mixture of experiential and genetic factors combined with being able to respond flexibly to the demands of changing environmental conditions.

Animal language

► Many animal species have communication systems which may have evolved through natural selection, such as signalling systems using visual, auditory, olfactory or tactile channels. Ridley (1996) says communication in animals performs an important function in mediating and organizing social behaviour.

► Words can be seen as a special kind of signalling system. Human language is a symbolic system governed by rules but, unlike many animal-signalling systems, it is extremely flexible and can convey a wide variety of meanings The question then arises whether any animal species have systems similar to this.

► Honey bee 'language' was researched by von Frisch in the 1940s. On detecting a food source, scout bees return to the hive and perform a 'figure of eight' and 'waggle dance'. The orientation of the dance relative to the vertical and the vigour of the waggles can be varied to convey the direction and distance of a food source to fellow bees. But is it language?

▶ Belding's ground squirrels use distinct calls to communicate the presence of different predators to each other. The behaviour patterns elicited by each call suggest an 'understanding' of the message.

▶ Chimpanzees have complex communication systems using vocalizations, facial expressions and movements which are useful for foraging, defence and attack and other social behaviours.

▶ Vervet monkeys have different alarm calls for eagles, leopards and pythons (Seyfarth and Cheyney, 1980). Learning appears to be involved in using these signals as young monkeys respond inappropriately to them more often than do adults, and monkeys in general respond differently to adult or juvenile alarm calls. The youngsters seem to be 'biologically prepared' to respond to particular categories of other creatures, such as flying ones, but have to refine their responses through experience and observation of other monkeys' behaviour. Marler (1987) sees such communication as an evolutionary link between signalling systems and human language.

▶ Grier and Burk (1992) say human communication is much more than even the most sophisticated animal 'language'. In our language, they say, 'Humans make extensive distinctions and references to other things, places, events and abstract concepts that may be external and far removed from ourselves in time, space, and even reality.'

Can animals acquire human language? Attempts to teach it to non-human animals seek to investigate:

▶ whether human language really is species specific; and
▶ whether non-human animals have thought processes as humans do.

Hockett (1960) suggested that human language has characteristics which he called 'design features'. Evidence of these in animals would support the idea that they can use language as humans do. There are sixteen design features, four of which are:

▶ displacement: reference to things not actually present in time or space;
▶ productivity: production of new words and an infinite number of novel utterances;
▶ prevarication: using language to talk about the ridiculous or impossible and to lie or tell jokes; and
▶ cultural transmission: language can be passed down the generations.

Gardner and Gardner (1969) attempted to teach American Sign Language (ASL) to a chimp called Washoe. She showed some similarities to human children's language acquisition, such as over-extending the meanings of signs and using two-word combinations. She also showed evidence of:

▶ displacement, e.g. by signing about things hidden in boxes;
▶ productivity, e.g. by making up new words such as 'water bird' for swan;
▶ prevarication, e.g. pointing to a green frog, signing 'that red', then rocking in apparent amusement; and
▶ cultural transmission. It is claimed that Washoe was seen trying to teach signs to her own baby.

Other well-known studies were carried out by Terrace (1979) who trained a chimp called Nim Chimpsky to use ASL, and Rumbaugh (1977) who trained chimps to communicate in 'Yerkish' using a keyboard of symbols.

Evaluation of animal language studies

▶ Terrace (1974) claimed that chimps used language very differently from children. They produced few spontaneous signs: in fact, it seemed that trainers were 'cueing' the chimps.

▶ He said that the chimps' sign order was often incorrect and repetitive as if they had no real understanding of what they were communicating.

▶ Chimps often interrupted their trainers and showed little evidence of being able to take turns.

A newer approach has been developed by Sue Savage Rumbaugh who teaches Bonobo chimps language from a large, portable signboard called a lexigram. Their coaching is much more like a child's would be. Instead of learning symbol by symbol, chimps pick up how to use the signs through:

▶ constant exposure to the trainer's example;

▶ using the lexigram themselves alongside all their daily activities; and

▶ hearing spoken language alongside all their activities

Even with this remarkably successful technique, the chimps' ability to produce language is limited (although, as with young children, their understanding of language outstrips their ability to produce it). Most researchers consequently agree that, although chimps can be trained in the rudiments of language production, they cannot acquire it with ease and speed or use it in the sophisticated way that humans do. Grier and Burk (1992) conclude that even if the difference between chimp and human use of language is only quantitative, the gulf is so large as to be practically qualitative.

Evolutionary explanations of human behaviour

▶ 'Evolutionary psychology is an attempt to make sense of human social behaviour ... within the framework of a set of rules derived from natural selection' (Archer, 1996).

▶ Evolution is a gradual process of genetic change over generations.

▶ Natural selection, first proposed by Darwin (1859), explains how evolution occurs. Individuals within a species differ genetically but the genetic mix of some gives them greater 'fitness' than others: they possess physical structures and behavioural patterns which mean they are better adapted to withstand the demands of their environment. They are more successful in surviving and reproducing, thus their genetic characteristics become more widespread in the population.

▶ Evolution may endow us with fixed characteristics but it also confers tendencies and dispositions within which a great deal of flexibility is possible. When a species finds a set of survival tactics that cannot be bettered, it is said to have an evolutionary stable strategy.

▶ The assumption that we are genetically pushed to survive and reproduce implies that we are inherently selfish. How, then, can evolutionary psychology explain cooperative and helpful behaviour such as altruism (helping someone else at apparent cost to oneself)?

▶ Inclusive fitness (Hamilton, 1964) is one explanation. The idea is that the more closely related we are to someone else, the more likely we will be to help them. In this way we can improve the fitness of individuals who carry similar genes to our own. This is borne out in studies which ask individuals who they would save in hypothetical life or death situations (Haldane, 1955). It can also explain why some children are at greater risk of abuse from step-parents than from their own parents and why xenophobia (hatred of strangers) occurs.

▶ Reciprocal altruism between unrelated individuals poses a special problem for evolutionary psychology which inclusive fitness cannot explain. The fitness benefit for the donor lies in having the favour returned later but there may be long delays in receiving fitness benefits and there is the risk of cheating (non-return of favours). Trivers (1971) suggested such helping is more likely in close-knit communities, where benefits are more likely to be returned and where cheats would be easily detected and unable to prosper. In addition, the helping of strangers is only likely when the costs are low and the potential benefits high. When individuals' fitness benefits coincide they tend to cooperate but when they do not, they tend to compete.

▶ Sexual selection refers to the selection of and differential access to sexual partners. It can be seen as a form of natural selection resulting in different physical and behavioural characteristics in the sexes, for example, in terms of reproductive strategies and degree of parental investment. It has been linked to polyandry and polygyny in human societies and to mate-selection in general. It has also been used to explain greater risk-taking in young men and jealousy in human relationships.

▶ Evolutionary psychology helps to broaden the base of psychology in general by bringing in historical and cultural elements. It can thus enrich other approaches such as social psychology.

▶ Many evolutionary explanations are based on inference and cannot be falsified empirically.

▶ Evolutionary explanations are useful but we must guard against over-determinism in using them to explain human behaviour. They are not the whole story and do not absolve humans from taking responsibility for their actions.

ESSAY QUESTION

Describe and evaluate evolutionary explanations of **two** aspects of human behaviour. *(24 marks)*
(AEB specimen question for 1997/8 new syllabus papers)

Bio-psychology

3

This chapter covers topics on states of awareness. In both waking and sleeping states we experience many different levels of awareness. The nature and functions of states of awareness are of concern to psychologists of all persuasions. Freud talked of the unconscious, the pre-conscious and the conscious. G. H. Mead (see Chapter 6) distinguished between the I and the Me as different states of awareness of self. Humanistic psychologists concentrate on understanding the nature of conscious experience. Early behaviourists rejected the study of mind altogether. Philosophers, too, speculate about the function of conscious awareness in general and the nature of the relationship between mind and body.

Here we concentrate mainly on the contributions of bio-psychologists. You will notice a great deal of overlap between some of the areas. Research into bodily rhythms in particular overlaps with theories of the nature and functions of sleep, so when writing essays on these topics you may be able to draw more widely than you think. But take care that you make your strategy explicit to the examiner.

TOPIC OUTLINES

Bodily rhythms, sleep and dream states

▶ Humans have many biological rhythms which seem to be adapted to the cycles of the Earth and which appear to be important for our survival.
▶ Humans seem to have both external (exogenous) and internal (endogenous) zeitgebers (time givers) which help to regulate our biological rhythms. Exogenous zeitgebers are both social (e.g. mealtimes) and physical (e.g. night and day). The supra-chiasmatic nucleus in the hypothalamus and the pineal gland, both in the brain, have been implicated as endogenous zeitgebers.
▶ In the absence of exogenous zeitgebers, rhythms become free-running and may desynchronize. Exogenous zeitgebers are needed to entrain and resynchronize disturbed rhythms.

Types of rhythm
▶ Circadian rhythms ('circa': about; 'dies': the day) roughly follow a 24-hour cycle. Humans have over 100 of these linked into the sleeping–waking cycle. For example, temperature fluctuates by about 3°F, peaking during the day and at its lowest at night; urine output decreases at night; hormones such as cortisol increase just before we wake.
▶ Infradian rhythms take longer than a day to complete. For example, the menstrual cycle in the human female averages 28 days and is governed by the release of chemicals such as follicle-stimulating hormone (FSH), luteinizing hormone (LH), progesterone and oestrogen. It is linked to the highly controversial idea of pre-menstrual syndrome. There may also be seasonal or circannual rhythms in humans. Wehr (1979) linked Seasonal Affective Disorder (SAD) to the reaction of the pineal gland (and other structures) to

lower exposure to full-spectrum light in winter.

▶ Ultradian rhythms occur more than once in 24 hours. Alertness seems to have a 90–100 minute cycle. There are many hormonal ultradian rhythms (e.g. FSH). The best known ultradian rhythms are the cycles which occur during sleep.

Stages of sleep

Waking, sleeping and dreaming have been studied mainly using the electroencephalogram (EEG) to measure electrical activity in the brain. Muscle activity can also be measured using an electromyogram (EMG), heart rate using an electrocardiogram (ECG) and eye movements using an electro-oculogram (EOG) to show how stages of sleep differ.

▶ When we are awake but resting, the EEG shows alpha waves of 8–12 Hz (cycles per second).

▶ In stage one sleep we become drowsy. Our metabolism begins to slow down and the frequency of alpha rhythms increases.

▶ In stage two, the EEG shows larger, slower waves of 3–7 Hz. Sleep spindles (bursts of activity of 12–14 Hz) and K complexes (two-second bursts of sharply rising and falling activity) occur.

▶ In stage three sleep, long, slow delta waves ($\frac{1}{2}$–2 Hz) make up to 50% of EEG activity.

▶ In stage four, the EEG shows almost entirely delta waves. Sleep is deep and quiet and metabolic rate very slow. It is difficult to wake a person from this stage.

▶ Stage one is also called 'desynchronized' sleep because of the irregular EEG. Stages two, three and four are called synchronized sleep. All four stages make up NREM (Non-REM) sleep.

▶ In the first sleep cycle, stages one, two, three and four are completed (about 30 minutes to one hour). The sleeper then reverses through stages three and two and then goes into active or 'paradoxical' sleep when the body is sleeping but the mind, as shown by the EEG, seems to be awake. There are increases and irregularities in heart-rate, blood pressure and respiration but the muscles are largely paralysed. Rapid eye movements occur in this stage, hence the name REM sleep. This whole cycle, from sleep onset, takes about 90 minutes.

▶ As sleep continues, we move from REM sleep to stages two, three and so on. REM periods increase in length. Eventually we descend only into the shallower sleep stages and we usually wake in REM.

▶ Aserinsky and Kleitman (1953) linked REM sleep to dreaming. About 70% of participants recall dreaming if woken from REM sleep. Further research has shown that we also dream in slow wave sleep but this is reported in only 30% of participants. These findings may be artefactual in that recall from REM sleep may be easier than from NREM sleep.

The physiology of sleep

▶ As darkness falls, the eyes inform the pineal gland which secretes melatonin.

▶ This stimulates the brain cells to produce a sleep-related neurotransmitter called serotonin.

▶ Serotonin concentrates in the raphe nuclei. These produce a chemical which acts on the Reticular Activating System (RAS): a structure which controls arousal levels. Light sleep ensues.

▶ Also implicated in sleep are the locus coeruleus and, possibly, 'Factor S'. The latter is thought to build up in the brain during waking hours, eventually leading to feelings of sleepiness.

Why is it useful to understand biological rhythms?

▶ The effects of drugs. Biological rhythms can affect the action of certain chemicals, making them more effective or even more dangerous. Halberg *et al.* (1960) found mice were more susceptible to toxins when asleep and more resistant to them when active during the night. In humans, timing the administration of medication to coincide with certain rhythms could render it more effective.

▶ Diagnosis of certain illnesses. This may rely on detecting substances in the blood or urine. Knowing how levels vary with rhythms could assist in improving the efficiency of diagnosis.

▶ Understanding the effects of disruption of rhythms (vital to minimize accidents and improve performance). Michael Siffre (1972) volunteered to spend six months alone in a cave free of all external cues depending only on his own free-running endogenous zeitgebers. His temperature cycle settled at around 24.8 hours and his average day was 33 hours. He slept longer if he went to sleep when his body temperature was high and less if he went to sleep when it was low. The desynchronization of his rhythms suggests more than one zeitgeber. Related to such findings are:

  – Jet lag. Moving across time zones can desynchronize rhythms leading to feelings of sluggishness and irritability and disruption of sleep and digestion, for example, trying to sleep when we would normally be awake coincides with cortisol levels and temperature being high or rising. All rhythms must be resynchronized and this happens more easily for some than others. This is easier if time is lost and rhythms must slow down rather than if time is gained and they must speed up. Klein and Wegmann (1974) recommend jet-lag sufferers engage immediately with the rhythms of life around them in order to adjust quickly.

  – Shift lag. In occupations requiring 24-hour staffing, changing shift patterns disrupt both family and social life and biological rhythms. For example, one week on and one week off can lead to constant feelings of exhaustion as some rhythms take up to a week to adjust and are then immediately disrupted again. In air-traffic controllers, whose job is already highly stressful, shift work and the consequent disruption of rhythms are added stressors. As with jet lag, shifting rhythms forward is more easily achieved but there are wide individual differences.

▶ Understanding certain mental disorders. Some kinds of depression are cyclic and associated with REM and NREM sleep being out of phase. Correcting sleep patterns has some short-term benefit, but the possibility of underlying disease linked to depression should not be overlooked.

▶ Helping insomniacs. 'Delayed sleep phase' insomniacs have problems getting to sleep but may eventually sleep well. One possible remedy is to move bedtime later and later until rhythms resynchronize with night and day.

▶ Contraception. The rhythm method of contraception uses, among other signs, rises in temperature which are associated with ovulation. It can be used both to help prevent pregnancy or to increase its chances of happening.

Theories of sleep

Restoration theory (Oswald, 1966)

▶ Sleep is seen as necessary for physiological and psychological repair and replenishment.

▶ In REM sleep the apparently higher frequency of dreaming suggests the restoration of cognitive functions through sifting, organizing and discarding new information from the day. (Babies have more REM sleep than adults.) Deprivation of REM sleep leads to REM rebound in which we catch up on lost REM sleep (Dement, 1960). A confounder in these studies is that participants woken as REM sleep starts go back into it more and more quickly, consequently they are woken more often and become more exhausted. Long-term effects of REM sleep loss are not evident, however, and we can adjust to sleep loss if it is a gradual process.

▶ In stage four sleep (a NREM stage) there is evidence of growth-hormone production. Deprivation of stage four sleep has been linked to lethargy, depression and increased pain sensitivity. Shapiro *et al.* (1981) found more stage four sleep in athletes who had just run marathons.

▶ Empson (1989) says no one can manage without sleep. Both physiological and psychological restoration probably occurs in both REM and NREM sleep, although one may predominate or be more easily demonstrable in one kind of sleep than in the other.

Evolutionary theory (Meddis, 1975)

▶ Many species show periods of torpid immobility associated with raised arousal threshold and changes in EEG.

▶ The theory says sleep increases the chances of survival by making us immobile and less conspicuous to predators. It also conserves energy and saves wear and tear. Hibernation is an extreme example. In contrast, preyed-upon animals who cannot hide themselves should sleep very little. (Unfortunately, this ability to explain both very little and a great deal of sleep in the same way makes the theory unfalsifiable.)

▶ Some critics (e.g. Empson, 1989) say that sleep-deprivation studies show there is more to sleep than simply wasting time in this way. All mammals and some non-mammalian species show some sleep-like patterns, suggesting it serves other important functions.

Dream theories (we sleep in order to dream)

▶ Freudian theory suggests that dreams enable us to fulfil wishes and fantasies in dreams and come to terms with our emotions. However, through 'dreamwork', the latent content of a dream is disguised. A trained analyst helps clients to understand the symbolism and other meanings of this manifest (recalled) content as one way of helping them come to terms with unconscious anxieties.

▶ The activation-synthesis model (McCarley, 1983) suggests that the brain cannot switch off completely during sleep and the periodic bursts of activity, along with other bodily sensations, are synthesized into a dream. Dement and Wolpert (1958) found that lightly spraying a sleeping person's face with water led to some form of incorporation of the experience into dreams.

▶ Reorganization of mental structures. Ornstein (1986) suggests we sleep in order to remember. Dreaming is the result of the work carried out by the brain to fit new information into existing mental structures or schemas. Sleeping on a problem often helps us to make sense of it.

▶ Dreaming to forget (Crick and Mitchison, 1983). During sleep we may sift, sort and discard information from the past, check circuits and generally clear out the system. This can explain why we may experience impressions from the previous day but not why we sometimes experience bizarre dreams with complicated storylines.

★ REVISION ACTIVITY • SLEEP AND DREAMING

On page 24 you will find a partially completed brain map on sleep and dreaming. See how many of the gaps you can complete from memory. Check your completed brain map against the solution on page 74 and then see if you can reproduce the whole thing from scratch.

Hypnotic states

'Hypnos' means 'to put to sleep' but the EEGs of hypnotized people show patterns similar to waking ones.

▶ There is speculation about whether hypnosis really is an altered state of consciousness.
▶ It is usually brought about through progressive relaxation and/or focusing on an object.
▶ Hypnotizability varies. Between 5 and 10% are not susceptible, 15% are highly susceptible and 75 to 80% fall in between.
▶ Hypnotizability can be measured by tests such as the Hypnotic Induction Profile which is based on the finding that hypnotizability correlates with the ability to roll the eyes upward (Spiegel, 1979).
▶ People with rich imaginations, a tendency to daydream and vivid mental imagery seem more susceptible to hypnotism. Evidence linking hypnotizability to other characteristics is mixed, for example, suggestibility does not seem to be a stable characteristic.
▶ People can utilize self-hypnosis for self-improvement.

Under hypnosis:

▶ planfulness ceases;
▶ suggestibility increases although it is thought that it is not possible to get a person to do absolutely anything – nor is it ethically reasonable to fully test this idea. People may regress, show anaesthesia, catalepsy and heightened or inhibited responses to certain stimuli;
▶ reality testing is reduced and reality distortion more readily accepted; and
▶ attention (to the hypnotist) becomes more selective than usual, although tests show that people's brains are still processing other incoming information.

Explanations

▶ Psychoanalytic theorists believe that hypnotic techniques release the unconscious mind from at least some of the conscious mind's control, hence the ability to regress, etc.
▶ Auto-suggestion may occur more readily in certain individuals, thus the outcomes of hypnosis may actually be placebo effects.
▶ State theories, for example, neo-dissociation theory, Hilgard (1973), suggest that hypnosis results from dividing the stream of consciousness into separate channels. Hence it is an altered state of consciousness.
▶ Non-state theories, for example, role-playing theory, Barber (1979), suggest we act out our expectations of certain social roles under social pressure from the hypnotist – and perhaps an audience too.

Research

▶ Pain relief. Atkinson *et al.* (1993) quote research to show that hypnosis can help in pain relief and that the degree of relief depends on hypnotizability. This may be because hypnotized people step up their production of natural painkillers (endorphins). However, using a chemical called 'naxolene' to block receptor sites for endorphins, Mayer (1979) found that hypnosis was still effective, therefore it must either work on a cognitive level or on another pain-blocking pathway.
▶ Post-hypnotic suggestion and learning. Lefrançois (1982) reported how a class was hypnotized and told they would understand and remember more of a lecture. Compared to an unhypnotized 'control' class they did indeed recall more but this could have been due to other variables induced by hypnosis such as greater motivation.
▶ Comparisons of hypnotized people and people simulating hypnosis produce

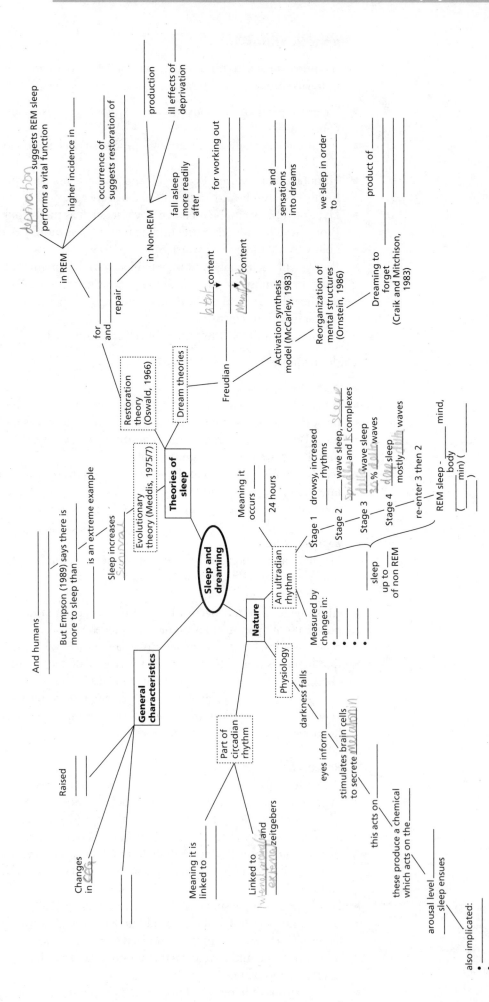

Figure 2: Sleep and dreaming: partially completed brain map.

interesting differences. For example, Evans and Orne (1971) faked a power cut half-way through a hypnotism session so that the hypnotist had an excuse to leave the participant alone for 30 minutes. Discreet observations showed the simulators stayed in a 'trance' for the full 30 minutes, while truly hypnotized participants gradually came round after about 20 minutes.

▶ 'Hidden observer' studies suggest part of the hypnotized person's mind can remain aware of what is happening to them. For example, it can be suggested to them, and demonstrated to onlookers, that they will only be able to hear when the hidden observer feels a hand placed on the shoulder. This is taken as support for Hilgard's (1973) neo-dissociation theory. However, not all hypnotizable subjects can produce a hidden observer.

▶ Hypermnesia (enhanced memory) has sometimes been claimed to operate under hypnosis. However, its use to improve eye-witness testimony is suspect, as such recall is open to distortions through the influence of reconstructive memory and leading questions.

ESSAY QUESTION

Describe and evaluate **two** theories of sleep. *(24 marks)*

Abnormal psychology

4

✓ REVISION TIPS

This chapter covers much of the material you will need on defining and classifying abnormality, different models of abnormality and cultural issues in this area. It is particularly useful to have a good grasp of models of abnormality because it will help you to understand other topics not covered here, such as explanations of specific conditions and the various therapies and treatments.

◎ TOPIC OUTLINES

Definitions and classifications of normal and abnormal behaviour

Defining normality

Normality is not simply the absence of abnormality. Atkinson *et al.* (1993) say it includes:

► efficient perception of reality;
► accurate self-knowledge;
► the ability to exercise voluntary control over behaviour;
► self-esteem and self-acceptance;
► the ability to form affectionate relationships; and
► productivity.

Defining abnormality

Questions in this area can be answered in a number of ways. Here are some suggestions:

► examine a variety of general approaches such as statistical rarity and deviation from the norm, sociocultural criteria, ideal mental health criteria and practical criteria (the latter including such signs as suffering and maladaptiveness);
► examine how classification systems are used to help define abnormality; and
► examine how the major approaches, such as the biomedical, psychodynamic and behavioural models, define abnormality.

The first of these is the approach most students use, although it would also be acceptable to roll all three together and go for breadth, rather than depth, or to emphasize one and mention the others to show that you can present an eclectic argument. (See the essay question and marked sample answer for this chapter on pages 75–76.)

Classifying abnormality

Practitioners have a variety of assessment techniques at their disposal, such as interviews or psychometric testing in order to help diagnose and classify disorders. The classification systems you are most likely to come across are the ICD 10 (1987) and the DSM IV (1994). DSM IV incorporates a diagnostic system based, at least in part, on identifying symptoms of mental disorder, such as their nature, onset, frequency, severity, duration and how they cluster together. The DSM IV is a mulitaxial system which means that, in addition to looking at symptoms, the individual is assessed on a number of dimensions, such as their physical state or recent experience of stressful life events. The two systems now have a great deal in common.

To answer questions in this area you will need to be able to summarize the main features of the ICD and DSM. It is not necessary to know them in every detail. An overview of the main categories is all you need (NEAB students should look elsewhere for information about assessment procedures and the problems they raise). You should then be able to address the practical and ethical implications of using such systems. (See outline answer to question 3, in the sample paper on pages 114–116.) Here are some points you could raise:

► Some of the practical strengths of classification systems are that they provide health professionals with a 'communication shorthand', they provide a theoretical framework for researchers to work from and they suggest something about the origin, likely course and treatment of a condition.

► Practical problems include establishing inter- and intra-observer reliability, establishing descriptive and predictive validity and taking account of biases that may affect diagnosis, such as across cultures.

► Another major practical consideration concerns the consequences of diagnosis in terms of treatment and how this may affect the individual.

► Ethical strengths could include the, hopefully, greater objectivity of the systems leading to less bias in diagnosis and more humane treatment of the mentally ill, no matter what their background.

► Ethical problems include 'labelling' and the question about whether this is a good thing (in that it helps the individual patient's understanding) or a bad thing (in that labels are 'sticky', or may become self-fulfilling). A wider view is taken by the 'anti-psychiatrists' – a movement that, among other things, expresses the view that mental disorders are not properly understood and to label them as 'illnesses' legitimizes society's actions towards the 'ill'.

Models of mental disorder

Models and treatments

Know the requirements of your syllabus here. The AEB and NEAB list the medical, behavioural, cognitive, humanistic and psychodynamic models and require you to know about the practical and ethical implications of these approaches. The revision exercise in this chapter will help you to do the following for each model:

► describe how it explains the origin of psychological disorders;
► outline the treatments deriving from it; and
► consider some of its strengths and weaknesses.

REVISION ACTIVITY • MODELS OF ABNORMALITY

On pages 28–29 you will find three lists of numbered terms and phrases and a table to organize them into. To start with, pencil a number where you think it belongs against each bullet. A number is used once only unless indicated in brackets. Continue until you have dealt with all the items, then check your solution on page 77. Now see how many you can recall unaided.

REVISION ACTIVITY • MODELS OF ABNORMALITY

Numbered terms to place in Table 3

Basic assumptions/terms

1 Emphasizes personal agency, individual freedom, basic goodness.
2 Disorders are biogenic.
3 Disorders stem mainly from neurotic anxiety.
4 Disorders result from infection, neurochemical factors, trauma, inherited systemic defects.
5 Behaviour is symptomatic of an underlying problem.
6 Blocks include failure to meet conditions of worth and gulf between ideal self and self concept.
7 Role of unconscious is central.
8 Disorders result from faulty cognitions.
9 Disorders result from learning maladaptive behaviour patterns.
10 Environmental determinism.
11 Fixations and ego defences can cause problems.
12 Reinforcement, punishment and extinction.
13 Disease model.
14 Faulty cognitions include irrational or upsetting thoughts, distortions of reality, maladaptive assumptions.
15 Blocks to personal growth and self-actualization cause problems.
16 Normal and abnormal behaviours are learned via conditioning and modelling.
17 Emphasizes role of early experience.
18 The symptoms are all there is to a problem.

Treatments and therapies

1 Client is responsible for own progress. (2)
2 A phenomenological approach is taken.
3 All approaches incorporate uncovering and restructuring cognitive processes.
4 Aversion therapy.
5 Can be combined with cognitive approaches.
6 Client and therapist work as a team.
7 Client must become aware of unconscious conflicts.
8 Dream analysis, free-association, parapraxes.
9 ECT.
10 Ellis' Rational Emotive Therapy.
11 Flooding and implosion.
12 Behaviour shaping.
13 Includes client-centred therapy (non-directive therapy) and group therapies.
14 Involves transference, interpretation, resistance, working through, catharsis and insight.
15 Meichenbaum's stress-inoculation training.
16 Psychoanalysis.
17 Psychopharmacology (including anxiolytics, anti-depressants, antipsychotics).
18 Biofeedback.
19 Psychosurgery (rarely).
20 Systematic desensitization.
21 Therapies are enabling and facilitating.
22 Therapists must show warmth, empathy, genuineness and unconditional positive regard.
23 Token economies.

Comments

1 Clients need to be verbally competent. (3)
2 Cultural bias. (2)
3 Firm basis in scientific research. (2)
4 Not effective on more serious psychotic disorders. (2)
5 Can be rapidly effective on less severe disorders.
6 Can be very time- and money-consuming.
7 Can explain the 'neurotic paradox'.
8 Combines well with behaviourist approaches.
9 Especially good on anxiety disorders.
10 Fosters helplessness and passivity.
11 Has contributed to better understanding of therapeutic relationships.
12 Lack of coherent theory makes testing difficult.
13 Lack of scientific backing.
14 Major successes with more serious disorders.
15 Optimistic and intuitively appealing.
16 Parsimonious.
17 Reductionist.
18 Scientific backing in cognitive tradition but still involves unobservable processes.
19 Symptom relief only?
20 Tendency to ignore inner person.
21 Tends to reject experimental approaches.
22 Underplays sociocultural factors.
23 Use of animals in research.
24 Uses classification systems.
25 Weeds out the cause of a problem.

Ethical issues in applying models of mental disorder

Clinical psychologists have developed a wide variety of treatments and therapies to help people with mental disorders. Some of the issues you might raise in examination answers in this area are suggested here. Remember to choose appropriate criticisms for a particular approach and to balance them with a consideration of how helpful and effective therapies and treatments can be:

▶ the vulnerability of people seeking help and the imbalance of power that may therefore result between client and therapist;

Table 3: Models of abnormality

Models	Basic assumptions/terms	Treatments and therapies	Comments
Medical (sometimes called biomedical or somatic)	▸ ▸ ▸	▸ ▸ ▸	▸ ▸ ▸ ▸ ▸ ▸
Behavioural Pavlov, Skinner, Bandura	▸ ▸ ▸ ▸ ▸	▸ ▸ ▸ ▸ ▸ ▸ ▸	▸ ▸ ▸ ▸ ▸ ▸ ▸
Cognitive Beck	▸ ▸	▸ ▸ ▸ ▸ ▸ ▸	▸ ▸ ▸ ▸ ▸
Humanistic Rogers, Maslow	▸ ▸ ▸	▸ ▸ ▸ ▸ ▸	▸ ▸ ▸ ▸ ▸ ▸ ▸
Psychodynamic Sigmund Freud (psychoanalytic approach)	▸ ▸ ▸ ▸ ▸	▸ ▸ ▸ ▸	▸ ▸ ▸ ▸ ▸ ▸

▸ the use of pain, deprivation and other aversive techniques especially in behaviour therapy;

▸ problems to do with systems of diagnosis and classification used by some practitioners, for example, concerns about their reliability, validity, cultural relevance and issues of 'labelling';

▸ concerns about whether clients can really give informed consent to treatments such as ECT when the reasons why they work are not fully understood, even by the practitioners;

▸ short- and long-term effects of biomedical treatments such as ECT, psychosurgery and chemotherapy;

▸ the choice of goals in therapies and treatments and different definitions of 'cure';

▸ wider consequences of treatment or therapy, such as changes to the person's life or relationships; and

▸ the view that therapies and treatments are simply another form of social control i.e. the focus on changing the individual which ignores the politically contentious possibility that it may be the social system rather than the person that is at fault.

Cultural and subcultural aspects of abnormality

Here are some points you could raise in essays in this area:

▶ First be clear about what psychologists mean by 'culture'. Triandis (1990) talks of 'cultural syndromes'. By this he means that a culture consists of a particular combination of beliefs, values, attitudes, norms and behaviours and that these distinguish it from other cultures. Within such cultures there may be further distinguishable subgroups or 'subcultures'.

▶ Western approaches to abnormality are based in Euro–American culture and consequently have a 'Eurocentric bias'. Within that culture there are subcultures defined by age, sex, social class or 'race'. Much psychological research is based on young, white, American men. Using a Eurocentric classification system based on such people is thus an 'imposed etic' which may not be valid in other cultures.

▶ The dominant culture tends to determine what is normal and acceptable behaviour and how problems are expressed, for example, in the US, overt acting out of behaviours is more usual than in certain Asian cultures. Failure to understand this could lead to Eurocentric bias in the diagnosis of Asians.

▶ The sociocultural model is especially useful here in emphasizing the role of social and cultural factors in determining how abnormality is defined. It raises questions of cultural relativity versus universality in various conditions. Traditionally, abnormal psychology has assumed there are universal mental disorders that cut across cultures and are largely manifested in the same way. This might be true of certain disorders, such as schizophrenia, but it does not readily apply to others, such as depression. Certain conditions (e.g. *windigo*, *koro* and *amok*) are specific to cultures and seem to be linked to folklore. Could *anorexia nervosa* be considered to be culturally specific?

▶ All the above points show the importance of taking cultural differences into account, otherwise a practitioner's Eurocentrism, personal stereotypes and prejudices could result in biases in diagnosis and classification. Some studies show practitioners allow their own biases, stereotypes and double standards to affect how they deal with clients (Sesan, 1988).

▶ Gender issues. Society places different values on what it thinks is appropriate for the sexes. Broverman and Broverman *et al.*, 1970 found that people's descriptions of a healthy adult are the same as for a healthy male but the descriptions for a healthy female are different from both – one cannot be both a healthy adult and female! More recent research shows less bias but there are still some concerns that certain categories in DSM may diagnose women as disturbed for acting out-of-line with the female stereotype. Women also receive more diagnoses than men of anxiety and depression and much more attention has been paid to premenstrual syndrome than to the role of males' hormones in mental health.

▶ Racial issues. Diagnosis of anxiety disorders is higher in African–Americans than in white Americans. Hispanics show more alcoholism. In the UK, Cochrane (1977) noted higher rates of diagnosis of schizophrenia in African Caribbean immigrants than for whites. Sue (1991) comments on the underuse of US mental health services by certain ethnic groups, such as Hispanic and Asian–Americans. The reasons could be financial but could also be caused by insensitivity to cultural issues on the part of therapists.

▶ Social class issues. The New Haven studies (e.g. Hollingshead and Redlich, 1958) showed that more members of lower socioeconomic classes appear in state mental hospitals. This could be for financial reasons but it could also be because lower socioeconomic groups express stress differently, for example, through aggressive and rebellious behaviour. Middle-class people tend to withdraw or become self-deprecating. Middle-class people tended to be labelled 'neurotic' and lower-class people the more serious 'psychotic'.

However, differential labelling cannot be the sole reason for these disproportionate numbers. For example, the lower classes may resist going for help for longer so their problems may be more severe. A developing mental disorder could also cause a person to drift downwards socially, swelling the numbers of disturbed people in the lower socioeconomic groups.

► Differential diagnoses according to gender, race or social class could result from real differences, or from stereotyping or ignorance on the part of the practitioner. This is a complex issue. Much research is only correlational. Sociocultural influences cannot be the whole story but they could set the scene for problems to take a hold.

► There are arguments both for and against diagnosis and classification. Systems must be consistent (reliable) and meaningful (valid) to be any use. They are imperfect but should, therefore, be improved rather than disposed of.

► What is the way forward? In diagnosis, practitioners must check the validity of their assessments especially when a client is from a different culture for which no norms have been developed. More and more research is being carried out into all kinds of bias in diagnosis and classification in an attempt to inform practitioners in this area and to develop culturally sensitive approaches. Practitioners must be helped to confront their own biases but a much wider programme of re-education is also needed.

ESSAY QUESTION

Describe and evaluate some of the ways in which psychologists have defined abnormality. *(24 marks)*
(AEB Paper 2, 1992, adapted for new mark scheme)

5 Cognitive psychology

Memory is a topic in cognitive psychology that many students find relatively accessible. In any case, research in this area is something you can readily apply to yourself when you are preparing for the examination! Syllabuses vary in the emphasis they put on different aspects of memory research and you will need to check the one you are following. But in general you should be conversant with:

▶ at least two models of memory e.g. two process theory, the levels of processing approach, reconstructive memory. You should also know about developments from these models;

▶ organization in memory (AEB students need to know this in some detail);

▶ ways in which your chosen theories of memory explain forgetting. This could include those listed above as well as explanations derived from schools of psychology, such as behaviourist, psychodynamic, Gestalt;

▶ practical applications of research into memory. The AEB syllabus *suggests* eye-witness testimony and memory for medical information although you could use other areas such as revision techniques or face recognition. The NEAB *requires* EWT and face recognition.

Remember that accurate, detailed knowledge of theory and research in these areas will earn credit but you need also to be able to evaluate these things and show that you have a good overview.

TOPIC OUTLINES

Models of memory

Atkinson and Shiffrin's (1968) multistore model of memory

▶ Memory is made up of a series of stores. These are the sensory information store (SIS), the short-term memory (STM) and the long-term memory (LTM). The stores differ in their encoding, storage and retrieval characteristics. This model is sometimes called the two-process model of memory because of the two major stores, STM and LTM. (See revision activity, pages 35–36.)

▶ Information transfers from STM to LTM as a result of rehearsal.

▶ Information in LTM is encoded in many forms. We know LTM contains knowledge, facts, beliefs, pictures, skills, language, and musical knowledge among many other things.

▶ There is a wealth of research evidence for the different characteristics of these stores drawing from experimental and physiological research (e.g. the case of HM).

▶ The model suggests rehearsal helps to transfer information into LTM but some studies show it is not essential. For example, we may remember parts of a lecture or a book simply because they are funny or interesting or relevant to us in some way.

▶ Baddeley (1986) has suggested that the STM was not just for the brief storage of information. He thought it also actively processed the information and decided what to do with it. His 'working memory model' has three parts: the articulatory loop deals with verbal information, the visuospatial scratchpad deals with visual information and the central executive decides how to share out the limited resources of STM.

▶ Atkinson and Shiffrin thought everything was held in the same LTM but this doesn't seem very likely. Other psychologists have argued we have more than one kind of LTM:

  – Mental imagery. Paivio (1971) carried out a great deal of research into this kind of LTM. It seems some of our LTM consists of 'images' from all our senses, such as visual images of someone's face, auditory images of the sound of their voice, olfactory images of the way they smell.

  – Declarative and procedural memory. Cohen and Squire (1980) suggest we have two LTM stores. Declarative memory stores things that we know. It is like a personal diary, dictionary and encyclopaedia all in one. We would use this memory to answer questions in a quiz or to tell a friend about things that have happened to us. Procedural memory is where we store knowledge of how to do things such as how to ride a bike, complete a jigsaw puzzle or hit a tennis ball.

▶ Atkinson and Shiffrin's model has been important in encouraging new research and theory about memory. The two previous points elaborate on the model rather than contradict it. The levels of processing approach however, offers an alternative view.

Craik and Lockhart's levels of processing theory

▶ Craik and Lockhart (1972) disagreed with Atkinson and Shiffrin's idea that memory consisted of separate stores. Instead, they suggested that memory depends on what we do with information when it comes in: in other words, how we process it.

▶ Shallow processing takes two forms. Structural processing is when we encode only the physical qualities of something. Phonemic processing is when we encode its sound. Shallow processing only involves maintenance rehearsal and leads to fairly short-term retention of information.

▶ Deep processing involves semantic processing which happens when we encode the meaning of a word and relate it to similar words with similar meaning. This means we are using elaborative rehearsal which leads to longer-term retention.

▶ Deep processing takes more effort and time than shallow processing and it could be this, rather than the depth of processing, that makes it more likely people will remember something.

▶ We do not know why deeper processing should aid memory. The levels model does not explain this.

▶ The levels model has been criticized for over-simplifying things so various changes and additions have been suggested:

▶ Elaboration. Craik and Tulving (1975) found that it was not just the depth of processing that affected retention but also the degree of elaboration a person carried out. For example, to just think of the definition of the word 'table' is deep processing but not very elaborate. We can elaborate 'table' more by thinking of different sizes of tables, made of different materials for different uses, thus making it more likely that we will remember 'table'.

▶ Distinctiveness. Eysenck (1979) suggested that if we can make something we want to remember stand out in some unique way we are more likely to remember it. This is because the memory trace is distinct from other similar ones and will not get confused with them. We remember some events, such as personal successes or disasters, because they stand out as being unusual or distinctive.

▶ Context. Tulving (1979) suggested that the setting (context) in which something is learned is encoded along with the material to be remembered. Stated simply, if we learn something in a particular setting we are more likely to recall it in that setting than in a different one, regardless of how deeply we processed it.

► Personal relevance. Rogers *et al.* (1977) found that participants who processed words in terms of whether they applied to them in some way (e.g. Do you own one of these? PARROT) remembered them even more than semantically processed words.

The constructivist approach to memory (Bartlett, 1932)

Bartlett suggested:

► We do not simply store a copy of something that we want to remember. Instead memory is seen as an active process. We construct our memories by combining existing knowledge with the new, incoming material. Retrieval involves reconstructing the resulting memories. It follows that people may remember quite different things about the same event because they have each constructed their memories in their own way.

► We will learn more about real-life memory if we give people meaningful things to memorize rather than lists of words. Bartlett used stories (e.g. *The War of the Ghosts*), faces and pictures in his tests of memory and found the following distortions: omissions, rationalizations, alterations in importance, changed order, added affect. Bartlett used the term 'effort after meaning' to explain this.

► Bartlett has given us an important alternative to other memory models by focusing more on memory as it is used in everyday life.

► The approach can be difficult to test because people's responses to the materials used are not easy to score.

► The approach causes us to consider how people differ in their recall of the same event. This is important in eye-witness testimony (see sample examination question and marked answer on pages 79–81).

► Bartlett's ideas have been developed into a 'cognitive approach to memory'. This approach asks what memory is for and how it fits in with other cognitive systems such as language and perception. Other approaches have focused more closely on the structure of memory.

Organization in memory

Research shows that memories are not stored in a random or haphazard way. Some form of organization is apparent and psychologists have speculated about its nature.

► Organization seems to operate at both the storage and retrieval stage. People sometimes actively organize material as they are committing it to memory. Spontaneous categorization of material at the retrieval stage is also evident.

► Bower *et al.* (1969) found that recall of large numbers of words was much improved if the words were categorized in advance. Giving people category names before the recall of disorganized lists also helped greatly.

► Collins and Quillian (1969) suggested that memories are stored in semantic hierarchies, i.e. interconnected, branching systems with many levels. They collected some evidence for this using sentence-verification tasks but there were some problems with this. For example, the time taken to respond 'false' to 'an ostrich is a fire engine' should be slow but is very rapid.

► Collins and Quillian (1975) suggested 'spreading activation theory' to overcome problems with sentence-verification tasks. They suggested that words differ from each other both in terms of semantic distance on a hierarchy and semantic relatedness.

► Bartlett (1932) suggested we possess a large number of schemata which enable us to take in information but the information may be distorted to fit. (See *The constructivist approach to memory* on page 34.)

► McClelland's (1981) parallel distributed processing model suggests that memories are stored in more than one place in interconnected units.

It is always worth remembering the phrase that 'to memorize is to have organized'. In this broader sense, any of the theories in Topic Outline 1 could be used to show how material is, for example, organized into different stores, levels or schemata.

Forgetting

Generally speaking this can result from failing to encode, store or retrieve adequately. The models in Topic Outline 1 can all be used to explain forgetting. A different angle can be offered if you consider how major schools of psychology explain forgetting e.g. psychoanalytic, behaviourist, Gestalt. (Also see Question Paper and Outline Answer on forgetting for this chapter.)

Applications of memory research

Four areas are suggested here:

► memory aids and revision techniques (see Revision Activity);

► eye-witness testimony (EWT) (see marked sample essay);

► memory for faces (see marked sample essay); and

► memory for medical information.

Various studies have been done to test how memory for medical information can be improved:

► Ley *et al.* (1973) found that presenting the structure of a message before it was given doubled recall from 25% to 50%, e.g. 'I am going to tell you three things: first what might be wrong, second what tests need to be done and third what will happen next.'

► Ley (1978) also compared patients' recall of what doctors had said against what was actually said. They found about 55% accurate recall. They also found evidence of a primacy effect, that repetition had no effect, that categorized information (for example, about medications) was remembered better and that patients with some prior medical knowledge recalled more.

► On the basis of these findings, Ley prepared an instruction booklet for doctors. Following the advice in this led to patients improving recall of information from 55% to 70%.

★ REVISION ACTIVITY 1 • MEMORIZING THE MODELS

1 Fill in the details for the two process and working memory models by placing the following terms in the correct places. Use a textbook if necessary.

Articulatory loop	Information lost as sensory image fades	Lasts up to 30 seconds
Capacity 5–9 items		LTM
Capacity 7 ± 2 items	Information lost for many reasons e.g. trace fades or lack of cues	Probably very large capacity
Central executive		Rehearsal loop
Could last indefinitely		SIS
Encoding	Information lost through interference or decay	STM
Encoding	Lasts 1–4 seconds	Visuospatial scratchpad

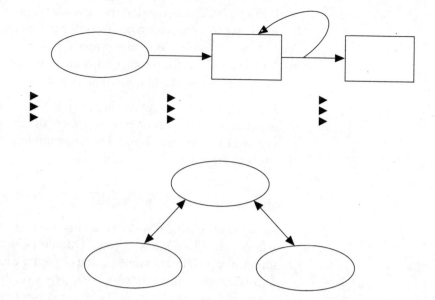

Figure 3: Atkinson and Shiffrin's Two-Process Model of Memory

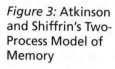

Figure 4: Baddeley's Working Memory Model

2 Levels of processing. Fill in the gaps in the following sentences:

> In 1972, Craik and Lockhart proposed that memory depends on how we process incoming information. There are two levels, _____ and _____ . The first of these takes two forms, _____ and _____ processing. Both of these involve _____ rehearsal and lead to _____ _____ retention. The second involves _____ processing, _____ rehearsal and _____ _____ retention.

3 Bartlett's constructivist memory model. Bartlett thought that, when we take in information, we may change it in certain ways to fit in with our existing schemata. Using stories such as *The War of the Ghosts* he found that the content changed in predictable ways. In the following Table, name the five kinds of changes that occurred and briefly explain each one and/or give an example. The first one has been done for you. Use a textbook if necessary.

Change	Explanation and/or example
Omissions	Certain details are left out in order to make the story flow better.
R	
A	
C	
A	

REVISION ACTIVITY 2 • MEMORY AIDS AND MEMORY MODELS

Models of memory can give us many ideas for improving recall. Look at the list of memory aids in the following Table, add in examples and the theory and/or theorist that you think they arise from.

Memory aid	Example	Background theory
Hook or peg system		
Method of loci		
Rhymes, phrases and stories		
Brain maps		
Preview, Question, Read, Summarize (PQRS)		
Re-check original sources		

ESSAY QUESTION

Describe and evaluate research findings into **two** applications of memory research, for example, eye-witness testimony, face recognition. *(24 marks)*

Developmental psychology

In this chapter we will cover theories of the development of morality, gender and self. Social learning, psychodynamic and cognitive developmental theorists have made contributions to all of these so you should know something about their basic principles. Here are some general points:

▶ Social learning theorists (e.g. Bandura, Mischel) think that we learn much of our behaviour through conditioning, but they emphasize *social* reinforcers and punishers, such as praise, attention, approval and disapproval. SLT's major contribution has been the study of observational learning or 'modelling' which helps to bring cognitive processes into the picture. It concentrates on human learning, particularly social and moral behaviour.

▶ Psychodynamic approaches such as those of Freud and Erikson emphasize unconscious forces in determining behaviour. Both these theorists think of personality development as occurring in a sequence of stages but whereas Freud emphasizes early experience, Erikson sees development as lifelong.

▶ Cognitive developmental theories such as those by Piaget and Kohlberg concentrate on the unfolding of understanding and reasoning which comes with age. They typically see development as occurring in a sequence of stages.

TOPIC OUTLINES

Moral development

Psychological theories of moral development are complementary rather than competing:

▶ Social learning approaches help to explain moral behaviour.
▶ Psychodynamic approaches are useful for explaining moral feelings.
▶ Cognitive developmental theories are best for explaining the growth of moral reasoning.

Theories of moral development
▶ Social learning theorists assume we learn moral behaviour through the same processes with which we learn any other behaviour: through conditioning and observational learning. Other people, such as parents, peers and teachers are vital in these processes. Over time, the initial external controls a child experiences become internal ones so other people are no longer needed to control the individual's behaviour. Classical conditioning explains how we learn the emotions we feel about moral or immoral behaviour. Operant conditioning can explain how moral behaviour is shaped and maintained. Observational learning can explain how we learn moral standards from models.

▶ Freudian psychoanalytic theory sees morality as developing in the phallic stage (4–7 years) as a result of the resolution of the Oedipal conflict in boys and the Electra conflict in girls. To resolve the conflict, children identify with the same-sex parent thus taking in many of that parent's characteristics including standards of right and wrong. Internalizing these results in the development of the superego. This has two parts: the conscience, which gives us guilty feelings if we do wrong, and the ego-ideal, which makes us feel worthy if we do right. Children with strict parents will suffer greater unconscious anxiety and have to work harder to resolve the conflict. The identification will be stronger and so will the superego. Girls do not experience as much unconscious anxiety as boys so their identification will be weaker and so will their superegos. Children in single parent families should be less moral because they do not have the chance to fully resolve their Oedipal or Electra conflict.

▶ Cognitive developmental approaches include theories by Piaget, Kohlberg and Gilligan. Piaget identified two main stages of development in moral reasoning. These are largely maturational. Heteronomous morality is shown by children up to 9 or 10 years old. Heteronomous means that their morality is controlled by others such as parents, teachers or other authority figures. Autonomous morality is evident in children over 9 to 10 years old. Autonomous means controlled from within. The child no longer needs others to say what is morally correct. Using stories such as the 'Heinz dilemma' Kohlberg (1969) identified three levels and six stages of moral reasoning. He suggested that children's moral reasoning could be encouraged by debating moral issues with others at higher stages of development. On Kohlberg's classification women tend to be scored as morally inferior. Gilligan (1982) suggested that this is because Kohlberg's theory is based mainly on research with males and is biased in their favour. She concluded that men and women are no different in their ability to reason about moral issues but women's moral reasoning centres more on care and men's centres more on justice. On Kohlberg's dilemmas, judgements based on care score lower than judgements based on justice.

Gender

'Sex' refers to a person's biological type: that is, male or female. 'Gender' is a person's psychological type: that is, masculine, feminine, androgynous or undifferentiated (Bem, 1975). Studies such as those of Maccoby and Jacklin (1974) tend to show far more psychological similarities than differences between the sexes.

Theories of sex-typing

The main problem for psychologists is to determine how biological and social influences interact in determining sex and gender. Bio-social explanations emphasize the role of factors such as genetics and hormones but also acknowledge the power of the environment in shaping how these are expressed. For example, Money (1972) found that ambiguous sex individuals must be correctly assigned to one sex as soon as possible, otherwise they may show inadequate sex-typing and be poorly adjusted.

▶ Social learning theorists think much of our learning can be explained by conditioning and observational learning. Sex-role and gender are learned by the same processes as any other behaviour. This process starts very early. Parents and others will selectively reinforce and shape gender appropriate behaviour in children. Also, models who are similar to the child, and who show gender appropriate behaviour, are more likely to be imitated. There are many such models for children to learn from, for example, teachers, peers, parents, images in the mass media. Different cultures also provide role-models. Margaret Mead's work with New Guinea tribes has been influential here but a more recent approach by Schlegel and Barry (1986) suggested that the male and female roles children were exposed to depended on the nature of 'food-getting'. Societies that gather food day-to-day tend to have less clearly differentiated roles, whereas food-accumulating societies tend to have more differentiated roles.

▶ Freud's psychoanalytic approach sees the development of gender as resulting from conflict resolution in the phallic stage brought about through identification with the same-sex parent. Identification means that the child internalizes many aspects of the parent's behaviour, including the expression of gender role. The stricter the parent, the more effort the child will have to make to resolve the conflict. This means the identification will be stronger, making boys more masculine and girls more feminine. Girls have weaker gender identities because the anxiety they experience is not as powerful as castration anxiety is for boys. This means less effort is needed to resolve the Electra conflict, so identification with the female sex is weaker.

▶ Cognitive-developmental explanations have been put forward by Kohlberg (1966) and Bem (1964). Kohlberg suggested that children need to develop an understanding of gender before they can take on a gender role. He suggested three stages:

1 Gender identity: 2–5 years, when a child can correctly identify themselves as a boy or a girl.
2 Gender stability: 4–6 years, when a child knows they always have been and always will be one sex only.
3 Gender constancy: 6–7 years, when a child understands that changes in dress or other kinds of appearance do not change a person's sex.

Bem suggests we develop a gender schema: that is, a mental structure which we use to take in knowledge about the world. A gender schema begins to develop as soon as the infant realizes there are males and females. From then on, the child will sort all new knowledge about people, their objects and activities into the schema under the general headings of male or female. Martin and Halverson (1983) suggest the development of the gender schema goes like this:

1 Children realize there is a male–female distinction.
2 They label themselves accurately as male or female.
3 At about 4–6 years of age they focus attention on observing their own gender.
4 At about 8–10 years old they will begin to pay more attention to the opposite gender so the schema expands to include more detailed information about both genders.
5 After this, the gender concept becomes more flexible: for example, girls know most boys don't play with dolls but they could if they wanted to.

The theory sees the strong sex-role stereotypes that children hold as a natural stage in the child's understanding of gender rather than something to be alarmed about.

Self

Attempts to define self-concept have led to some confusion. 'Self' or 'self-concept' are terms which encompass:

▶ Self: our conscious awareness, centre of experience, sense of existence, the subjective self or 'I'.
▶ Self-concept: the self-image or ego-identity, the set of ideas we have about ourselves, the 'Me'.
▶ Self-esteem: how we feel about our self and whether we evaluate it negatively or positively.
▶ Ego-ideal: this is how we would like to be.

Generally speaking, a change in any one of these could bring about a change in the others, so the 'self' is not so much a static 'thing' but more of a 'process'.

The following diagram illustrates how the various components fit together.

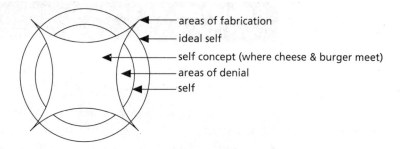

Figure 5: A Self
Cheeseburger

Tests of self-recognition in infancy (e.g. Lewis and Brooks-Gunn, 1970) have demonstrated that self-recognition is evident as early as 9–12 months. A sense of self may develop earlier than this, but since we are dependent on drawing inferences from infants' behaviour, there is, as yet, no way to be sure.

Theories of the development of self

Among the major theorists there is general agreement that the infant does not see itself as having a separate identity. It develops a sense of self over time:

▶ In SLT the sense of self arises from interactions with others as the infant begins to link its actions with their reactions. The infant becomes aware that s/he is an 'agent' that can make things happen in a world separate from itself.

▶ Another approach with a social emphasis is G. H. Mead's symbolic inter-actionism. He thought that a sense of self develops with time through social interactions with others. He distinguished the 'I', which is the basic sense of self-awareness, from the 'Me' which is the sense of self as an object to others. To develop the Me we learn to reflect on ourselves just as we reflect on others. This ability develops through primary socialization in childhood when we learn to mentally take the role of others and see ourselves as they see us. Secondary socialization takes over later on. Examples of this include feedback from significant others, comparisons with others and the roles we play.

▶ In Freudian terms the infant does not see itself as separate from its mother. Eventually, the ego develops and it becomes necessary to acknowledge the existence of a social world outside oneself which makes certain demands and has certain expectations. The psychodynamic theorist Erikson (1968) suggested that, in adolescence, the crisis to be faced is 'identity versus identity diffusion' from which the young person should emerge with a firm sense of identity. Marcia (1980) went on to identify four identity statuses: identity achievement status, foreclosure status, moratorium and identity diffusion. In adulthood we progress through still more psychosocial stages and our experiences in these affect our overall sense of self.

▶ In Piaget's view, the infant gradually loses its profound egocentrism. The arrival of object permanence at about eight months plays a part in this and is an essential precursor to understanding person permanence and self-permanence. The infant soon starts to use terms of self-description and of possession, such as 'mine'. In early childhood, it can be demonstrated that children can decentre and see things from another person's point of view. Cognitive developmentalists tend to see self as being largely established in childhood and incorporating various aspects of self such as gender identity (explained by Kohlberg, 1966). However, there is disagreement about the timing of development. A great deal of new research suggests infants' and children's understanding of self comes about much earlier than Piaget suggested.

REVISION ACTIVITY • BRAINSTORM ON MORAL DEVELOPMENT

You will need to draw more widely than this chapter to answer some of these questions. Suggested answers can be found on pages 82 to 83.

1 Give three reasons why punishment may not be effective in teaching moral behaviour.

2 Why do social learning theorists say parents should practise what they preach?

3 What are the two parts of the superego called and how do they make us feel?

4 What is the main difference between heteronomous and autonomous morality?

5 What would Piaget have called these types of punishment applied to a child caught stealing money from a parent's wallet:
  (a) The parent should steal the same amount from the child's piggy bank.
  (b) The parent should take the child to the police.
  (c) The parent should stop the child from seeing friends that day.

6 In the Table below arrange the following examples of moral reasoning into order according to Kohlberg's three levels and six stages:
  (a) Heinz should steal the drug or his wife will die and won't be able to look after him.
  (b) Heinz shouldn't steal. If he's caught he'll go to prison.
  (c) Heinz should steal the drug. His wife's life is more important than anything else.
  (d) Heinz should steal the drug or he'll never forgive himself.
  (e) Heinz should steal. It's against he law but this is a special case.
  (f) Heinz should steal the drug. Everyone will think he's very brave.

LEVEL	I		II		III	
STAGE	1	2	3	4	5	6
STATEMENT (Insert letter)	b	a	f	d	e	c
	Punishment & obidence	Instrumental relativist	Interpersonal concordance	law & order	legalist/ social contact	Universal ethical principles

7 According to Gilligan, how do men and women differ in the basis of their moral judgements? — They don't. He found no difference.

8 Make two evaluative statements for each of the following theories of moral development:
  ▶ Social learning theory;
  ▶ Freudian theory;
  ▶ Piaget's theory;
  ▶ Kohlberg's theory; and
  ▶ Gilligan's theory.

ESSAY QUESTION

Discuss the role of social factors in the development of gender. *(24 marks)*

Theoretical perspectives and philosophical issues

REVISION TIPS

This section covers five major perspectives on psychology and five philosophical issues. These underpin almost everything you study on your A- or AS-level psychology course because they comprise the fundamental assumptions different psychologists make about the nature of human behaviour and how best to understand it. There will be many occasions when you can use information from these central topics in your examination answers. The obvious times are when you are answering questions explicitly dedicated to them. The less obvious times are when you are analysing or evaluating in a specialist area, for example, in considering ways of treating psychological disorders. A good way to do this is to examine the soundness of the underlying psychological theory and assumptions on which your answer is focusing. They are the foundation on which the knowledge rests and, if it is not sound, neither is that particular knowledge.

The five perspectives dealt with here are:

▶ the psychodynamic approach;
▶ the behaviourist approach;
▶ the humanistic approach;
▶ the cognitive approach; and
▶ the biological approach.

Most introductory psychology courses treat these five perspectives (and more) as being distinct from each other. This is generally for the sake of clarity so that you can appreciate them in their 'pure' form and see where the more modern approaches have originated. Present-day psychology often mixes them together, for example, in social learning theory, cognitive developmental psychology, cognitive behavioural therapy or the bio-psychosocial approach to health. Many psychologists welcome this merging of perspectives because it gives psychology such richness and diversity. There will probably always be a place for the 'pure' approaches but they can happily coexist with newer, more eclectic, ones and help to enrich each other.

A good way of offering evaluation of a perspective or issue is to bring in opposing views which, perhaps, make up for the gaps in the approach that the question has asked you to focus on. You should always make it obvious that you are bringing in alternative views for the purpose of evaluation, otherwise the examiner might think you have lost sight of what you are doing. Questions on perspectives can be asked in a number of ways. You should be prepared to:

▶ write on any specified perspective;
▶ compare and contrast perspectives; and
▶ discuss how different perspectives relate to different philosophical issues (see Revision Activity 2 on page 48).

Note: If you are an AEB student, your syllabus states that you *must include* the psychodynamic, behaviourist and humanistic approaches in your studies. It does not specify others but you would be well advised to look over the cognitive and biological approaches to help you with other areas of the syllabus. NEAB students need all five perspectives and OCSEB students would benefit from reading over all five.

The five philosophical issues to be covered are:

► freewill and determinism;
► reductionism;
► nature and nurture;
► idiographic and nomothetic approaches; and
► objectivity and subjectivity.

You will need to know the nature of the five issues and their implications for the way in which behaviour is subsequently explained and studied. Although psychologists have sometimes been known to adhere to an extreme position on one or more of these issues, it is more often the case that they could be placed somewhere between the two extremes.

TOPIC OUTLINES

Perspectives

The psychodynamic approach
One of the clearest examples of the psychodynamic approach is the psychoanalytic theory of Sigmund Freud (1856–1939). Freud's followers (e.g. Jung, Erikson, Klein) developed his theory and changed some of its emphases but they continued to share some of the original assumptions.

Basic assumptions
► Much of our behaviour is biologically determined by the unconscious operation of instinctive forces.
► Although our biological make-up is important, early experiences are also influential and can have a profound effect on later behaviour.
► Personality develops in stages and, although the sequence is universal, the individual's early experiences result in a unique personality.
► The fully developed personality consists of an id, an ego and a superego.

Methods
► Freud based much of his theory on clinical case studies but he also drew on knowledge of different cultures.
► Freud developed techniques for tapping into the unconscious mind, including free-association, analysis of dreams and 'Freudian slips' and examination of his clients' sense of humour, accidents and forgetting.
► Later theorists have developed projective tests consisting of relatively unstructured materials on to which clients project meaning.

Contributions
► Freud attempted to produce a universal theory of human behaviour so the contributions of this approach have been very wide-ranging. The theory can explain abnormal behaviour, personality development, dreaming, accidents, forgetting, humour and the appeal of great works of art.
► The therapeutic approach known as psychoanalysis and developments from it are useful in clinical settings.
► The theory's wide appeal has led to the incorporation of many of its key ideas into Western culture and to many new theoretical developments.

Comments

▶ The theory has been criticized for not being readily amenable to scientific testing and, in particular, for being irrefutable.

▶ Its apparent negativity about the prospects for normal healthy development, its view of women as secondary to men and of infants and children as 'polymorphous perverts' have all attracted criticism.

▶ The subjectivity of its methods mean that much of the basic ideas are the result of Freud's own interpretations.

The behaviourist approach

This approach is said to have originated when J.B. Watson published a paper in 1913 entitled *Psychology as the Behaviourist Views It*. Watson was dissatisfied with approaches such as Wundt's structuralism and Freud's psychoanalytic approach, both of which focused on unobservable phenomena and subjective interpretation. Instead, Watson argued that psychology should concentrate on observable behaviour and attempt to study it scientifically. In fact, early behaviourists rejected the idea of studying mental processes altogether as they were not directly observable. Other important theorists in this area are Pavlov (1849–1936) and Skinner (1904–1990).

Basic assumptions

▶ Humans are essentially biological organisms but they have a great capacity to learn from experience, hence most of their behaviour is environmentally determined through conditioning.

▶ The basic unit of learning is the S–R (stimulus–response) connection.

▶ Humans can be seen as related to other animals through evolution, therefore much of human behaviour can be understood by studying the behaviour of less complex species.

▶ It is possible to discover general laws of learning which apply to both animals and humans.

Methods

▶ Behaviourists advocate the scientific study of behaviour under carefully controlled (often laboratory) conditions.

▶ Laboratory studies of learning in animals such as rats, mice and pigeons underpin much of what we know about human learning although human participants are obviously also used.

Contributions

▶ Behaviourism has helped to raise the profile of psychology as a scientific discipline by offering a parsimonious, objective and empirical approach to studying behaviour.

▶ Like the psychoanalytic approach, behaviourism has given us an extremely wide-ranging theory to explain many different aspects of learned animal and human behaviour, ranging from the development of aversions to certain foods through to the acquisition of complex skilled behaviour such as driving a car.

▶ It has given us powerful techniques for changing behaviour in a wide variety of settings, particularly in education and in clinical practice.

▶ The influence on psychological thinking has been considerable. In particular, traditional behaviourism has given rise to newer approaches such as social learning theory and cognitive behavioural approaches which bring mental processes back into the picture.

Comments

▶ Some critics think behaviourism has overemphasized environmental determinism and argue that we exercise considerable freedom and choice about how to behave. Nevertheless, Skinner argued that free-will is an illusion and that all behaviour is controlled by environmental forces to some extent.

▶ Some critics say that the emphasis on the objective study of human behaviour is inappropriate, arguing that the mechanistic view of the person is dehumanizing.

▶ Anti-extrapolationists argue that it is unjustifiable on practical grounds to transfer findings from animals to humans – and some people object to the use of animals on ethical grounds.

▶ The techniques behaviourists use to change behaviour can be seen as coercive and controlling. This has led to criticisms on ethical grounds.

★ REVISION ACTIVITY 1 • THE HUMANISTIC APPROACH

Following the format already used in outlining the psychodynamic and behaviourist perspectives, complete the following Table using the humanistic perspective. If you are an NEAB student, you will also need to be able to do this for the cognitive and biological perspectives. Suggested solutions are given on pages 85–89.

Table 6: The humanistic approach

General points and major contributors

Basic assumptions

Methods

Contributions

Comments

Free-will and determinism

Psychologists who adopt a determinist position think that people's actions are the result of forces over which they have no control. These could be internal causes, such as instinctive forces, or external causes, such as conditioning experiences. In this view, behaviour is never random or capricious. An extreme free-will position is that people have absolute personal control over everything they do, consequently their behaviour is entirely unpredictable and not amenable to being studied scientifically. Extreme psychoanalytic and behaviourist views are examples of biological and environmental determinism respectively. Humanistic psychologists are closer to the free-will position but would not accept that behaviour is entirely without cause or unpredictable. It is more a matter of degree. The position between the two extremes is sometimes referred to as 'soft determinism' and most psychological approaches would find themselves located between soft determinism and determinism.

Reductionism

Reductionism is the view that behaviour can be better understood by breaking it down into its constituent parts. Behaviour is seen as resulting from these parts working together. The most extreme form of reductionism is to see behaviour as resulting from the activity of sub-atomic particles but reductionist psychologists do not usually take such an extreme view. Instead, they use whatever level they think is appropriate to give an adequate account of behaviour. Early behaviourists thought that S–R connections were adequate to explain behaviour. Physiological psychologists might use the level of activity of hormones or the nervous system, cognitive psychologists might reduce the person to the level of an information-processing machine and social psychologists might explain social behaviour at the level of the individual. One problem with reductionism is that 'the whole is greater than the sum of its parts', hence reductionist explanations rarely give a complete account of behaviour. A solution to this is to adopt an interactionist perspective and try to explain behaviour in terms of how different levels work together.

Nature and nurture

This concerns the debate over the extent to which behaviour is determined by heredity or environment. Nativists, for the nature side, argue that behaviour is genetically predetermined and, if it is not evident at birth, it will develop through maturation. Empiricists, for the nurture side, argue that behaviour is determined by experience and that, without an appropriate environment, certain behaviours will not develop. The truth probably lies between these extremes with some behaviours being relatively more influenced by heredity, and therefore less malleable, than others. This interactionist position is supported by a number of lines of evidence. PKU, for example, is an inherited disorder, the potentially damaging effects of which can be averted through an appropriate diet. A number of abilities seem to be genetically programmed to develop, through experience, during a 'sensitive period' and will not develop if this sensitive period is missed. In classical conditioning, we seem 'biologically prepared' to learn some associations more easily than others.

Idiographic and nomothetic approaches

Idiographic approaches prefer to focus on individuals on the grounds that each person is unique. The nomothetic approach is aimed at discovering general laws of behaviour that apply to everyone. The scientific method fits well with the nomothetic approach which seeks general laws of behaviour that can be used to predict how people will behave. The idiographic approach tends more towards individual approaches, such as the case study from which generalization to others could be possible but may not always be so. The nomothetic approach is more in line with reductionism and the idea that cause and effect can be discovered in behaviour whereas the idiographic approach emphasizes the study of the whole person exercising (relatively) free choice over how to behave. Ultimately, it is perhaps more useful to see the two approaches as complementary. The idiographic approach is especially useful at the start of the scientific process of gathering knowledge where we are at the stage of wanting to describe our subject matter and make predictions about it. The nomothetic approach comes into its own later on when we want to be able to predict and control behaviour.

Objectivity and subjectivity

Objectivity is to do with whether it is possible to understand human behaviour by studying it from the point of view of a dispassionate observer whose observations are free from bias. The idea is that it is somehow possible to understand behaviour as it really is, just as one would be able to understand non-human objects or events. Subjectivity is the view that people can only be fully understood through the study of their individual experience and their descriptions of the meaning their own behaviour has for them. The judgement of a 'third party' observer is, therefore, unnecessary. Objectivity sits fairly comfortably with the view of psychology as scientific; subjectivity does not. However, humanistic psychologists argue that objectivity is a myth. No scientist can be truly objective, so all 'scientific' knowledge is ultimately subjective.

REVISION ACTIVITY 2 • THEORETICAL PERSPECTIVES AND PHILOSOPHICAL ISSUES

On pages 49 and 50 there are two Tables. In the first Table you will find the five philosophical issues, each with five chunks of information relating to that issue. Taking each row in turn, decide which chunk of information describes the point of view taken by each of the five perspectives and enter it in the correct box in the second Table. A good way to check your understanding would be to proceed as follows:

► Take each issue in turn and rearrange the five related chunks of text to where you think they belong. At this stage, lightly pencil in the numbers (1, 2, 3, 4, or 5) corresponding to the relevant chunk of text into the second table.
► When you think you have it right, check your solution against the Table on page 89 and make any necessary corrections.
► Now cover the first Table and write a summary of the text into the second Table from memory. Check your answers when you have finished.

ESSAY QUESTION

Discuss contributions of the behaviourist approach to psychology. *(24 marks)*

Table 7: Theoretical perspectives and philosophical issues   Statements to unscramble into Table 8

Issues	1	2	3	4	5
Freedom and determinism	Behaviour is mainly environmentally determined through conditioning experiences, although some biological determinism occurs through genetic limitations on ability. (Pigs can't fly!)	Past experiences count but people are generally free to choose how to behave based on their assessment of a situation. They are responsible for their own behaviour.	Behaviour is biologically determined by the operation of primarily sexual and aggressive instinctive forces, although early experiences also affect how we behave.	Behaviour is doubly determined (genetically and environmentally). People have no choice over heredity or environment and these factors interact to produce behaviour.	Behaviour is 'freely determined' in that there is some selection and interpretation of stimuli and some decision and choice, but these operate within the constraints of how the system is organized.
Reductionism	Reductionism operates on a number of levels. The most basic is to explain behaviour in terms of the structure and function of the nervous system.	An extreme form of reductionism applied here is 'machine reductionism' where the system is seen to operate on input like a computer (with hardware and software).	This approach is an example of biological reductionism (seeing instinctive forces as driving behaviour).	Reductionism is rejected in favour of 'holism' which advocates the study of the whole human being.	An early view in this approach was that behaviour could be reduced to S–R associations. Later views incorporate cognitions.
Nature and nurture	Shared biological type (nature) means that humans are all motivated by the same need to achieve their potential, but life (nurture) can help or hinder this.	Nature and nurture cannot be separated. The organization and operation of the brain and how we process information are affected by both.	Nature and nurture are inseparable. They determine our physical make-up and interact to produce behaviour.	Innate biological forces (nature) are paramount but early experiences interact with these to shape personality.	Environmental experiences are paramount (nurture) although our physical make-up will impose limitations.
Idiographic/ nomothetic	Idiographic. This approach studies unique individuals seeing them as architects of their own lives.	Nomothetic. General principles of structure and functioning that apply to everyone are sought.	Nomothetic. General principles of structure and functioning that apply to everyone are sought.	Nomothetic. This approach attempts to discover laws of behaviour which are generally applicable to all.	Idiographic and nomothetic. Individuals have personalities based on their unique experiences but the course of develop-ment is nomothetic (generally applicable to all).
Objectivity/ subjectivity	Objectivity. The adoption of the scientific approach is central to this approach, hence the emphasis on objectivity.	Objectivity. Stemming from the view of humans as biological machines, whose structure and function can be studied objectively to see how they relate to behaviour.	Objectivity. This springs from the original view of humans as machines whose structure and function can be viewed in an objective, scientific way.	Subjectivity. The individual's subjective experience is more important in understanding behaviour than an outside observer's interpretations.	Subjectivity. This stems mainly from the use of clinical case studies which are used to gather subjective reports. These are then subjectively interpreted.

Table 8: Theoretical perspectives and philosophical issues

Issues	Perspectives				
	Psychoanalytic	Behaviourist	Humanistic	Cognitive	Biological
Freedom and determinism					
Reductionism					
Nature and nuture					
Idiographic/ nomothetic					
Objectivity/ subjectivity					

Ethics

In revising this topic you will need to be careful that you are familiar with the emphasis put on ethics in your syllabus. The AEB devotes a whole, compulsory subsection of its syllabus to ethics and will set essays in this area. Both the AEB and the NEAB emphasize them in their compulsory sections on research methods and in connection with abnormal psychology. The OCSEB lists ethics as one of its underlying themes and expects candidates to be able to use them to evaluate other areas of the course content. As with perspectives, philosophical issues and methodology, ethics are important in many areas of psychology. They can therefore be used in many contexts as a means of evaluation, even if they are not explicitly asked for in a particular question.

The most obvious places you will encounter ethical considerations are:

▶ in psychological research using human participants (the AEB adds 'socially sensitive' research);
▶ in the application of psychological knowledge (see abnormal psychology in Chapter 4); and
▶ in psychological research using animals (explicitly on the AEB syllabus; also useful for others).

In all these areas, it can be tempting to adopt a 'moral high ground' and to argue from an extreme position. Examiners will credit any well-reasoned argument but it is advisable to offer as balanced an account as possible to show that you are aware of different viewpoints.

TOPIC OUTLINES

Psychological research using human participants

Ethics are moral standards and rules of conduct that guide psychologists and others in their work. In the field of research with human participants, you should, as a minimum, be able to:

▶ list the content of a set of relevant ethical guidelines such as those offered by the British Psychological Society (BPS) or the Association for the Teaching of Psychology (ATP) and know the specific ways in which the guidelines can be followed. This will give you a framework on which to hang any essay on ethics in such research;
▶ outline at least two examples of research with human participants that have received more attention than most for ethical reasons;
▶ identify ethical issues raised in these examples and consider whether they could be resolved; and
▶ arrive at a considered conclusion about the costs and benefits of your chosen research examples.

REVISION ACTIVITY 1 • ETHICAL CONSIDERATIONS IN PSYCHOLOGICAL RESEARCH WITH HUMANS

This activity is to help you to meet the minimum requirements set out in the Topic Outlines. The BPS research guidelines and Milgram's work on obedience to authority are used here. Use the table of guidelines to complete the second table explaining and commenting as much as you can. Issues raised in the study itself are marked with a ✓; others are marked with a ✗.

When you have completed the table, look at the suggested solution on page 93. A solution for Zimbardo *et al.*'s prison-simulation study, on which you could do the same exercise, appears on page 94. You could try other studies: Asch's classic work on conformity, Piliavin's field research on bystander behaviour on the New York subway, Bandura's Bobo doll studies, Ainsworth's 'strange situation' research, the case of Little Albert, Rosenhan's work *On Being Sane in Insane Places* or Rosenthal and Jacobson's *Pygmalion in the Classroom* study. Most general textbooks for A-level psychology will include accounts of these.

Socially sensitive research

This is an issue specifically named on the AEB syllabus but students following other syllabuses should also find it useful for evaluating certain research studies. Sieber and Stanley (1988) define socially sensitive research as: 'studies in which there are potential social consequences or implications either directly for the participants in research or the class of individuals represented by the research'. By this they mean that, when the research findings become generally known they could be used to justify discrimination against certain groups or even changes to social policy. This could amount to a kind of 'social control': findings are used to uphold dominant social values which may not be in the best interests of the individual. Examples include:

▶ Milgram and Zimbardo *et al.*'s research (outlined in Revision Activity 1);
▶ Freud's psychoanalytic case studies and the conclusions he drew from them about women and children in particular;
▶ Mead's anthropological research into child-rearing styles;
▶ Bowlby's classic work into mother–infant attachment; and
▶ Burt's work on IQ concordance in twins and any other research into the role of genetics in determining any aspect of behaviour.

Psychologists who carry out socially sensitive research run particular ethical risks but may argue that it is their moral responsibility to conduct such studies especially if they help disadvantaged groups. However, there is no ethical code of conduct for such research or guidance about how to deal with the consequences. Sieber and Stanley (1988) recommend that ways are found to prevent the abuse of potentially sensitive research findings wherever possible. Psychologists themselves must develop a heightened sensitivity to the potential impact of their findings especially on social and cultural groups different to their own. For example, they need to be aware that much of psychology has a 'Eurocentric' (American–European) bias and may not be applicable to other cultures whose values and lifestyles are different.

Look again at the list of studies above and for each one consider the possible social consequences for:

▶ the actual participants in the research; and
▶ the type of person represented by the research participants.

There are few definite answers to this. It is up to you to discuss your ideas with others and to speculate as creatively as you can.

Table 9: Ethical guidelines for research with human participants (1993)

Guidelines	Explanation	Comments
1 General	Investigators must consider the ethical implications and psychological consequences for research participants bearing in mind ethnic, cultural , social, age and sex differences.	Check design with members of the population from which the participants are to be selected. If this isn't possible, ask people who can act on their behalf.
2 Consent	Obtain consent from participants whenever possible, preferably 'informed consent', i.e. explain, as fully as possible, the purpose and design of the research before proceeding.	If the procedures are likely to involve physical or psychological discomfort, the researcher must seek the guidance of colleagues before asking for consent.
3 Deception	Avoid this wherever possible. There will occasions when to reveal the research hypothesis to participants would make the research pointless and so deception would be considered.	Do not use if there is an alternative procedure. If deception is planned, consult with others about it, e.g. individuals similar to the participants, colleagues and ethics' committees.
4 Debriefing	This must be 'active intervention', i.e. the psychologist must be ready to discuss procedures and findings with participants and try to ensure that they are left in the same state in which they entered the research situation.	Intention to debrief participants is no excuse for exposing them to risk, neither is the inability to debrief them (e.g. as in some observational research).
5 Withdrawal from the investigation	Participants must be told of their right to withdraw, without penalty, at any stage of the research. Researchers must stop any procedure which appears to be causing discomfort.	This may be difficult to achieve (e.g. in observational research). After debriefing, participants have the right to withdraw their data.
6 Confidentiality and privacy	The Data Protection Act 1984 means that participants can expect that their identities and any information provided by them will be treated confidentially.	Psychologists have a duty to break this guideline if not to do so would place someone at great risk. A fully informed participant may give consent to their identity being revealed.
7 Protection of participants	Protection of participants from mental or physical harm during psychological investigations including invasion of privacy is essential.	Must show great sensitivity in discussion of results with participants. They should know how to contact the investigator if an unexpected consequence of the research arises. The researcher must correct or remove the problem.
8 Observational research	It is important to respect people's privacy and wellbeing especially as it may not be possible to obtain informed consent or debrief participants.	Make observations only where people would normally expect to be in public view and not where they expect to be unobserved.
9 Giving advice to participants	A researcher may uncover a significant psychological or physical problem. This must be revealed to the participant and professional help advised.	Few research psychologists are expert enough to spot problems! They should only offer help themselves if they are appropriately qualified.
10 Monitoring colleagues	Investigators have a moral responsibility to maintain high ethical standards and should monitor their own work and that of colleagues.	This applies at any level of research. All research projects need to be carefully assessed on ethical grounds before proceeding.

Table 10: Revision activity 1: Ethical considerations in Milgram's obedience to authority study (1974)

Outline of a study. Milgram obtained a varied, volunteer sample of 40 men to take part in a study allegedly about learning and memory. During the study, elaborate deceptions were necessary to convince participants that they were giving increasingly powerful electric shocks to another person. Participants were encouraged to continue in this even when they protested, the true purpose of the study being to see how far they would be prepared to obey the researcher's authority.

Ethical guideline (BPS, 1993)	Comment
1 ✓ General	1
2 ✓ Informed consent	2
3 ✓ Deception	3
4 ✓ Debriefing	4
5 ✓ Withdrawal	5
6 ✓ Confidentiality and privacy	6
7 ✓ Protection of participants	7
8 ✗ Observational research	8
9 ✗ Giving advice	9
10 ✓ Monitoring colleagues	10

Concluding comments e.g. Did the ends justify the means? Could Milgram have designed the study differently?

Psychological research using animals

If you are an AEB student, you could be asked to write an essay on this topic. Other students may find that they can use the issues raised here to evaluate any topic incorporating research based on animals. As a minimum you should be able to:

▶ give examples of the wide variety of methods psychologists use in animal research;
▶ comment on the incidence of animal research in the UK and USA;
▶ outline practical arguments for and against the use of animals in psychological research;
▶ give some examples of applications of psychological research using animals;
▶ comment on the current legislation and ethical guidelines concerning animal research; and
▶ summarize ethical arguments concerning animal research and attempts to resolve the issues raised.

REVISION ACTIVITY 2 • PSYCHOLOGICAL RESEARCH AND THE USE OF ANIMALS

On page 95 you will find a brain map expanding on the points listed above. Study it well, then cover it and see if you can fill in the blank brain map on page 56 from memory. If you can find your own examples where asked for, or elaborate the brain map, so much the better. Suggested reading: Wadeley, A., Birch, A., Melim, A. (1997) *Perspectives in Psychology*, London: Macmillan.

ESSAY QUESTION

1a Outline the main ethical considerations involved in psychological investigations using human participants. *(12 marks)*
1b With reference to **two** studies, assess attempts made by psychologists to resolve these issues. *(12 marks)*

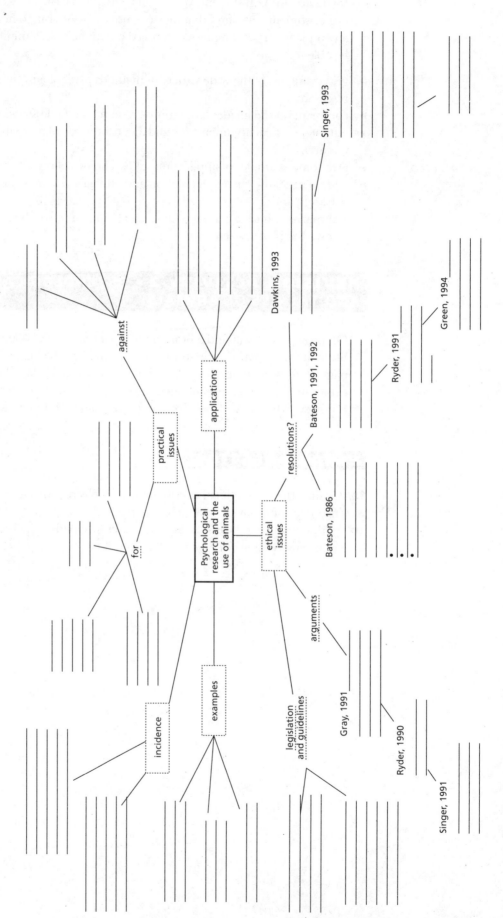

Figure 6: Psychological research and the use of animals: partially completed brain map.

9 Methodology, research design and statistics

REVISION TIPS

METHODOLOGY

Your knowledge of psychological research methods is most likely to be examined in the context of other questions. The place where this will certainly happen is in the compulsory methodology and data analysis questions. However, as with all 'core' topics, you should be able to bring methodology issues into many other answers. A good way of assessing the worth of any theory or piece of research evidence is to examine the research methods that were used. All methods have strengths and weaknesses (and some psychologists apply them more competently than do others!). Consequently, the soundness of a theory or research finding can always be examined in the light of these things.

In the heat of the examination, you certainly do not want to find that you are unclear about the terminology used by the examiner so here are some pointers:

▶ Experimental and non-experimental methods. A formal definition of an experiment is: 'A research method in which an IV is varied so that its effects on a DV can be observed and measured. All extraneous variables are held constant.' The experiment is the only method that allows us to talk about cause and effect. By this definition, all other methods are non-experimental. There is a 'fuzzy' area, however, concerning quasi- and natural experiments in which the IV is not under the experimenter's direct control. Some people argue that such methods are more observational than experimental.

▶ Laboratory and non-laboratory (field) research. A laboratory is any research environment that is closely controlled because it has been set up by the researcher. Non-laboratory research tends to take place in a more naturalistic setting, perhaps one that is familiar to the research participants.

▶ Quantitative and qualitative research. Quantitative research involves measuring amounts of something, or otherwise counting or predicting, using statistical data. Qualitative research tends to involve more subjective interpretation of the meaning of such things as participants' verbal reports or discourse.

REVISION ACTIVITY 1 • PSYCHOLOGICAL RESEARCH METHODS

A table of research methods has been set out for you on pages 58–59. Your task is to add information from memory and/or using textbooks wherever you see an asterisk *. The purpose of this exercise is to ensure that you can describe psychological research methods, illustrate them with examples and comment on the strengths and weaknesses of each method. A complete version of the table can be found on pages 100–101. The answers given there are suggestions only. You may have made different but equally valid ones.

Table 11: Psychological research methods

Method	Description	Example	Comments
Observation	*		* * *
Non-participant observation	Observing from 'outside', taking a 'fly on the wall' approach. Can be ▶ * ▶ *	Ethological studies e.g. of territoriality. *	* Less control but greater ecological validity. *
Recording techniques include: ▶ baby biography and diary description;	Detailed written description of behaviour often in infants and children.	*	Rich accounts but object-ivity harder to achieve.
▶ specimen description;	*	'One Boy's Day', Barker and Wright (1951).	As above, and could be unrepresentative.
▶ event sampling	Recording incidences of a particular kind of behaviour, its context, ante-cedents and consequences.	Bell and Ainsworth (1972). Mothers' responses to infant crying.	**
▶ time sampling.	Recording behaviour in specified, regular segments of time.	*	*
Participation observation	*	Festinger et al. (1956) infiltrated 'The Seekers' a quasi-religious group who believed the world was about to end.	* Potentially rich and detailed understanding of group but danger of becoming a 'non-observing participant'.
Case Study	An in-depth study of a single instance of something. It can be a study of * It is an idiographic method aimed at gaining a detailed understanding of the individual case.	Many examples can be quoted e.g. Allport's work on personality, Freud's psychoanalytic case studies, **	Uses a variety of data-collection methods, all with inherent strengths and weaknesses. * * * Not always readily generalizable but a number of similar case studies could be.
Surveys	Used for gathering data from large numbers of people using questionnaires and interviews. Questionnaires can contain ** and be completed face-to-face, by post or by telephone. Interviews can be ***	Attitude surveys e.g. Sears Maccoby and Levin (1957) on child-rearing styles; The Hite Report (1977) on female sexual behaviour; *	Difficulties with devising unambiguous questions that avoid bias, 'leading' the respondent or causing offence. ** *
Correlation	Not a research method in itself but a widely used statistical technique for detecting * in samples of paired data. Such analysis can be applied to data collected in a variety of ways. Correlation coefficients vary from **	Widely used in * studies e.g. genetic resemblance studies of IQ or the incidence of certain mental disorders. Can be used to show links between early experience and later behaviour e.g. in media violence research or *	* Useful for detecting patterns that may suggest new hypotheses for experimental testing. *
Psychometric testing	The measurement of psychological attributes such as intelligence or personality using various testing techniques and usually yielding * data.	IQ tests such as ** Personality tests such as **	Tests must be reliable, valid and standardized. * Best used as part of overall assessment. *

(Continued)

Table 11 *Continued*

Method	Description	Example	Comments
Content analysis	A way of making qualitative information quantitative perhaps by setting up categories into which instances of events can be counted.	Used to examine content of media (e.g. Cumberbatch, 1990) or of **	Helps to make qualitative data available for statistical analysis. * *
Experiment	Manipulation of IV in order to observe corresponding changes in DV while holding extraneous variables constant. Includes: ▶ * ▶ field experiment; ▶ * ▶ natural experiment.	Many examples can be drawn from behavioural, cognitive, comparative and bio-psychology. ▶ IV and research environment controlled; ▶ * ▶ IV occurs naturally, environment controlled; ▶ * } **	Enables us to identify * Must be aware of confounding variables. Can be criticized for being dehumanizing.

Research design and statistics

The approach taken in this chapter is not to provide you with a mini-textbook on research methods and statistics but to alert you to key concepts on which you may be examined. Until you see the examination paper you will not know what context to set your answers in, so you must be prepared to think on your feet and adapt the material presented here accordingly. Questions often offer some stimulus material followed by questions requiring short answers. Some of these questions relate directly to that material; others require you to draw more widely from your knowledge. By far the best preparation is to practise answering questions. The marked example will give you a good idea about the amount of detail required for the marks available.

The stimulus material will describe fictitious studies that are either experimental or non-experimental. If statistical analysis is involved it will be a test for differences, correlation or association. It helps if you can be clear about these two things before you start. You can also expect to be tested on both your understanding of research design, which includes ethical issues (see Chapter 8) and statistics. You will not be required to remember complicated statistical formulae or carry out the tests themselves, although you may be asked to work out an average, interpret a correlation coefficient or decide whether a test result is significant. All the information necessary for you to do such things would be in the stimulus material.

Before we start on what you need to know, remember that research design and methods questions are just as important as the essay questions. You should give them as much attention as the essays and not leave them to the last ten minutes. Even if the thought of research methodology and statistics leaves you cold, take heart from the fact that much research design is common sense. The answers to some of the questions will be very straightforward and obvious but if you're not sure, have a go! You may get it right. Examiners do not penalize wrong answers and they work hard to credit what they can. If you haven't even tried to answer a question, zero is all they can give.

REVISION ACTIVITY 2 • RESEARCH METHODOLOGY AND STATISTICS

Before you complete some practice questions from past papers, work through the following questions. The answers are provided for you but don't look at them yet. See how much you can do from memory. You may be surprised at how much you have picked up simply by carrying out coursework. When you have done all you can, look at the suggested answers and make sure you understand them. Perhaps you could get a friend to test you by firing some of the questions at you at random. This should give you a clear indication of what you still need to learn. Once you feel reasonably confident, try the sample question and use the mark scheme and sample answers to see how you got on.

GENERAL METHOD QUESTIONS

1. What is an experiment?
2. What is the difference between an experiment and a correlation?
3. What is an independent variable (IV)?
4. What is a dependent variable (DV)?
5. What is a confounding variable?
6. What is an extraneous variable?
7. What is a control group?
8. Distinguish between independent groups, matched pairs and repeated measures designs.
9. What are practice effects?
10. What are order effects?
11. What is counterbalancing?
12. What is randomization?
13. Write out an hypothesis for a study comparing imagery and repetition as aids to memory.
14. Provide a null hypothesis to go with it.
15. What is a directional hypothesis and when would it be used?.
16. What is a non-directional hypothesis and when would it be used?
17. When would a one-tailed test be applied?
18. When would a two-tailed test be applied?
19. Suggest two ways in which aggression could be operationalized.
20. What are demand characteristics?
21. What are experimenter effects?
22. What is meant by participant reactivity (subject effects)?
23. What is a single blind procedure and why is it used?
24. What is a double blind procedure and why is it used?
25. What is meant by a population in psychological research?
26. What is meant by a sample in psychological research?
27. Give two reasons for sampling.
28. How might you take a random sample?
29. What factors determine sample size?
30. Name and define two sampling techniques other than random sampling.
31. What is meant by reliability?
32. Name and define three different kinds of reliability.
33. What is meant by validity?
34. What is experimental validity?
35. What is ecological validity?
36. Name and define three further kinds of validity.
37. In what two senses is the term standardization used?

38 What are standardized instructions?
39 What is a pilot study? What is the purpose of pilot studies?
40 What is (a) a cross-sectional and (b) a longitudinal research design?

STATISTICS QUESTIONS

41 Sketch a normal distribution and give three adjectives to describe it.
42 Sketch three other shapes of frequency distribution.
43 What are measures of central tendency used for?
44 Name and define three measures of central tendency.
45 When would you use a median rather than a mean?
46 What are measures of dispersion used for?
47 Name three measures of dispersion.
48 What is a z-score?
49 Name four levels of measurement.
50 Between which two values can a correlation coefficient vary?
51 Is a correlation of -0.8 weaker than a correlation of $+0.8$? Explain.
52 What does df stand for?
53 Express $p = 0.05$ in words in two (or three) different ways. Do the same for $p = 0.01$. Now try $p < 0.05$ and $p \leq 0.05$. Now try $p > 0.05$ and $p > 0.01$.
54 Why is the 0.05 significance level often used in psychological research?
55 What is meant by a Type I error and how is it dealt with?
56 What is meant by a Type II error and how is it dealt with?
57 Complete Table 12 'Selecting appropriate tests'.
58 Which three assumptions underlie the use of a parametric test?
59 With reference to parametric tests, what is meant by 'robustness'?
60 With reference to parametric tests, what is meant by 'power efficiency'?

Note: Questions 48 and 58 to 60 are essential for NEAB students and optional for OCSEB and AEB students.

Table 12: Selecting appropriate tests (AEB students need only complete the bottom row)

| | Experiment | | Correlation | Association |
	Related design	Independent design		
Data suitable for a parametric test				
Data suitable for a non-parametric test				

EXAMINATION QUESTIONS

AEB specimen module Paper 7 section B or terminal Paper 3 section D. Allow 45 minutes.

Question 4
(a) Give **two** ways in which the laboratory experiment and the natural experiment could be considered different. *(2 marks)*
(b) State **two** limitations of conclusions that might be drawn from natural experiments. *(2 marks)*
(c) What is meant by *naturalistic observation*? *(1 mark)*
(d) Briefly outline the main factors that a researcher must consider when choosing to use the naturalistic observation technique. *(3 marks)*

Question 5

A researcher wishes to explore the influence of peers on cognitive development in children aged between six and ten years. She intends to do this by using interviews with children, questioning them on their views of moral problems such as whether or not it is acceptable for a child to cheat in a classroom test. The researcher intends to use a team of four colleagues to interview children in a group with peers and on their own.

(a) Describe an appropriate way in which the researcher might select the children to take part in the study. (*2 marks*)

(b) Justify the use of either an independent group, repeated measures or matched pairs design. (*3 marks*)

(c) Explain how you would maximize reliability in the study. (*3 marks*)

Question 6

A researcher wished to investigate the relationship between participants' performance on two attentional tasks. One task involved responding to a series of stimuli with no other stimuli present (the control condition). In the second task, a further set of stimuli was introduced (the divided attention condition). Five trials were carried out on each participant. The scattergraph below shows the results obtained.

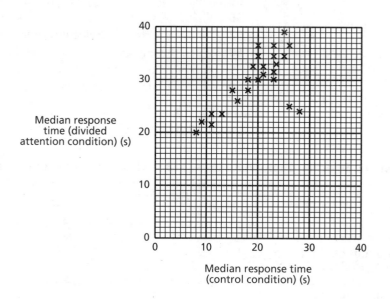

(a) What is meant by the term *median*? (*1 mark*)

(b) In what circumstances might the median be preferred as a measure of central tendency? (*2 marks*)

(c) What conclusions can be reached from examining the scattergraph? (*2 marks*)

(d) The psychologist who produced the scattergraph wished to ascertain if there was a relationship between the two sets of scores. Suggest one statistical test that might have been employed to do this and give reasons for your choice. (*3 marks*)

(Total 24 marks)

part III
Answers and grading

Skill A material has been differentiated from Skill B material:
Skill A is presented in ordinary type, while Skill B appears in italics.

Solutions
Social psychology

SOLUTION TO REVISION ACTIVITY

See Brain map on page 66.

ESSAY QUESTION AND MARKED SAMPLE ANSWER

Critically consider psychological explanations of social power in relation to leadership. *(24 marks)*

> **Examiner's note** The injunction in the question invites both Skills A and B and these are equally weighted. You should show knowledge and understanding of your chosen theories and research evidence for A and an awareness of their strengths and weaknesses for B.

What makes a good leader? Are some people born to lead? When considering this, there are two major appoaches that we can look at in the search of evidence.

> This isn't what the examiner has asked for. A better approach might have been to clarify what is meant by 'leader' and 'social power'.

According to the trait approach, certain people have characteristics that allow them to rise to positions of power. Cowley (1928) believed they would be well-adjusted, self-confident, intelligent and attractive in appearance. Bass (1990) believed that an energetic and sociable personality was important and that a certain amount of intelligence was necessary to become a leader. *But studies have shown that a typical leader has only slightly higher intelligence than others in the group. Researchers could not identify significant characteristics that leaders possessed and their followers did not. There seemed to be no list of consistent key traits. According to Brown (1985), although personal qualities are important, it is also important to consider leadership qualities in relation to the situation and problems to be faced by the group. In other words, certain traits will be needed in one situation and different ones in another.*

The situational approach looks at leadership as a role. It acknowledges that leadership involves leaders and followers in various role relationships. Rather than having certain personality characteristics, a leader will be the person who possesses the skills and information most relevant in a given situation. *This approach, however, does not take into account the extent to which the leader is effective and does not allow for the fact that followers can affect their leader's behaviour and therefore a social process is involved. Transactional theory does look at leaders and followers in relation to each other.*

Fiedler's contingency model can be used to explain what kinds of leaders exercise the most power in which situations. He asked leaders to indicate their least preferred co-worker (LPC) in a group. Leaders who talked of the LPC in negative terms were more task-oriented and those who talked of the LPC in more positive terms tended to be more person-oriented or socioemotional.

Socioemotional leaders would be better under normal conditions. Task-oriented leaders would work better under extremely good or poor conditions but under normal conditions, their cooler relationship with individuals would work against them.

Fiedler has reported considerable support for his model but some studies have shown that the orientation of the leader is not fixed. Even the gender of the leader is important in some situations regardless of whether it is favourable or unfavourable or the leader is task or person-oriented. Perhaps this model focuses on the personality of the leader too much, although it does take account of the social nature of leadership and that situational factors are involved.

> These are three well-known explanations of leadership but they need to be more explicitly linked to the idea of social power. There is a good attempt to evaluate the trait approach but the evaluations of the situational approach and contingency model need to be explained more carefully.

We can also look at leadership style to see how it affects how influential a leader is. Lewin *et al.* (1939) investigated the effect of three types of leader on 10-year-old boys. The adults were either:

1 Autocratic: they told the boys what to do. They were friendly but impersonal. The boys in this group became aggressive to each other and stopped work as soon as the adult was out of sight.
2 Democratic leaders: these discussed what the boys would be doing and allowed them to choose who to work with. The boys made their own decisions with guidance from the adult. They were generally more interested in the task at hand and carried on working and cooperating when the adult left the room.
3 *Laissez-faire* leaders – they were friendly but left the boys to do as they liked and offered little help. The boys had little interest in what they were doing and were apathetic.

Lewin *et al.* found that democratic leaders worked best overall but the autocratic-led groups produced more overall. *This suggests that the style of leadership matters more than personality but it could be that a particular personality expresses itself as a particular style of leadership so perhaps the two are not so far apart. If this is successfully mixed with a given situation, the leader could be very influential. In conclusion it is important to take traits, style and situation into account to explain when a leader will be powerful.*

> This is a useful section with some good description and quite a complex evaluation. There is still a tendency to avoid the issue of social power and what it really means.

> Over all, this is a well-organized essay with relevant material on the emergence and effectiveness of leaders which could have been used to much greater effect. The candidate needs to state explicitly what they understand by social power (perhaps using a general definition and French and Raven's categories) and then go on to show ways in which it might be linked to leadership before evaluating the chosen material. Credit is given here for useful content and a good balance of reasonable evaluation. 14 out of 24 marks. (Skill A, 9 marks: bottom of Band 3; Skill B, 5 marks: bottom of Band 2.)

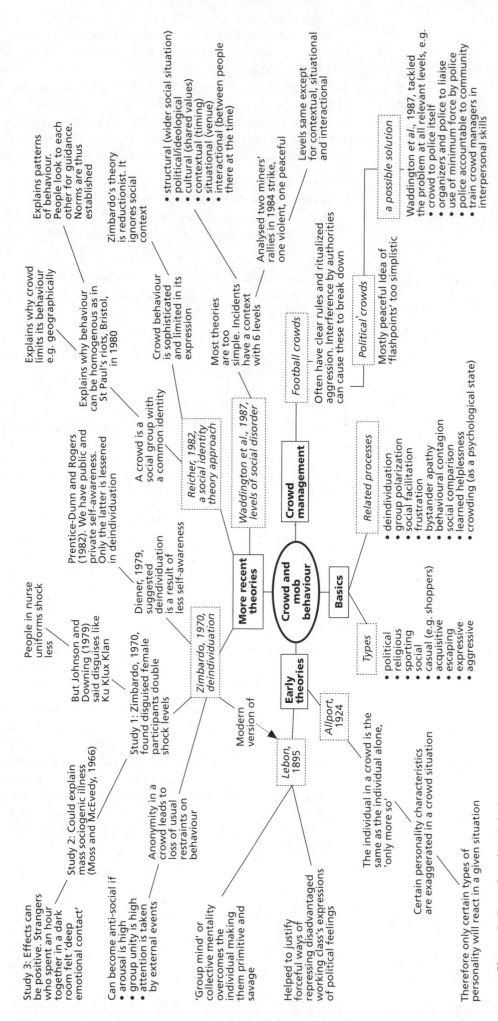

Figure 8: Crowd and mob behaviour: completed brain map.

Solutions
Comparative psychology

SOLUTIONS TO REVISION ACTIVITIES

Revision activity Brainstorming conditioning theories

1 What sorts of behaviour does classical conditioning explain best?
Fears, phobias, other emotional reactions and food aversions.

2 Define the term 'reflex'.
An automatic response to a stimulus.

3 Draw diagrams to show how classical conditioning could account for:
(a) a child's fear of men in white coats.

Unconditional reflex   UCS ⟶ UCR
                pain from medical treatment   fear

Conditioning trials   NS   +   UCS ⟶ UCR
              white coat   pain from   fear
                      medical treatment

Conditional reflex   CS ⟶ CR
                white coat   fear

(b) an adult's aversion to lemon meringue pie.

Unconditional reflex   UCS ⟶ UCR
                viral or bacterial infection   sickness

Conditioning trials   NS   +   UCS ⟶ UCR
              lemon   viral or bacterial   sickness
              meringue pie   infection

Conditional reflex   CS ⟶ CR
                lemon meringue pie   sickness

4 To what might a classically conditioned fear of budgerigars generalize?
To stimuli like budgerigars e.g. other small birds or feathered creatures.

5 How might you train a dog to discriminate between rectangles and squares?
Using the standard Pavlovian procedure and mixing trials in which food
(UCS) is presented along with squares but not with rectangles.

6 What kinds of learned behaviour does operant conditioning explain?
It is particularly good for explaining the acquisition of skilled behaviour that
is shaped and refined with time, for example, maze learning in rats.

7 How would you use shaping to teach a rat to pick up a marble and drop it
into a cup?
Using behaviour shaping by successive approximations. The rat would be
selectively reinforced for making responses which came closer and closer to
the desired behaviour.

8   Distinguish between negative reinforcement and punishment.
    Reinforcement is any event which has the effect of increasing the likelihood
    that a particular response will follow a stimulus. Punishment is any event
    that is aversive or unpleasant and which has the effect of suppressing
    responses to stimuli.

9   Define the term 'extinction'.
    This refers to the disappearance of conditioned responses following
    non-reinforcement.

10 Give one example each of latent learning, insight and learning set.
    ▶ Tolman (1930) showed how rats who had been allowed to explore a maze
      without reward seemed to develop a cognitive map of the maze to use to
      good effect when reward was introduced into the goal box.
    ▶ Köhler (1925) showed how apes could spontaneously solve the problem of
      stacking boxes to reach a banana (the 'Eureka' or 'Aha' effect) as opposed
      to trial and error.
    ▶ Harlow (1949) showed how chimps could develop learning sets for finding
      food rewards (e.g. the food is under the shape which is the odd-one-out)
      and then transfer the set to new situations.

11 Explain the role of expectancies in conditioning theories.
    Expectancies were introduced into newer versions of conditioning theories
    to help explain the role of cognitions in the learning process. Bindra (1968)
    said that in classical conditioning, animals learn an expectancy that a UCS
    will follow a CS. Bolles (1979) said that, in operant conditioning, animals
    develop an expectancy that a particular consequence will follow a response.
    In both cases animals can adapt their responses accordingly.

12 Explain the term 'instinctive drift' and briefly say why it challenges
    traditional conditioning theory.
    Instinctive drift is a term coined by Breland and Breland (1961). For
    advertising purposes, they tried to train pigs and racoons to pick up 'coins'
    and drop them into money boxes. The animals proved impossible to train:
    the pigs drifted back to their instinctive tendency to root the coins along the
    ground and racoons drifted to rubbing the coins between their paws as they
    would their natural foodstuff.

ESSAY QUESTION AND MARKED SAMPLE ANSWER

Describe and evaluate evolutionary explanations of **two** aspects of human
behaviour. *(24 marks)*
(AEB specimen question 1996)

> Examiner's note: The Skill A marks for this question are for showing
> knowledge and understanding of evolutionary explanations of the two
> aspects of human behaviour that you have chosen. Skill B marks are for
> making an informed judgement about the value of these explanations.
> There are many aspects of human behaviour to choose from, such as
> territoriality, apparent altruism, aggression, parental behaviour. The
> chosen two areas should be carefully described from an evolutionary point
> of view. Evaluation could focus on theoretical and methodological issues.
> Alternative explanations or studies of the same aspect of behaviour in
> non-human animals can be used as evaluation, providing you take great
> care to justify their inclusion.

First it is essential to explain what is meant by the evolutionary approach to explaining human behaviour. Evolution is the process by which the genetic make-up of a species changes over generations. This happens, as Darwin suggested, by natural selection. Darwin thought that all species could over-reproduce but that there were insufficient resources to support ever increasing numbers of animals. It follows that there will be a struggle for survival which only certain individuals will win. Those who win will be the ones who are the best adapted to cope with the demands of their environment or ecological niche. Darwin also talked about 'fitness' which could be measured by the number of offspring the animal left behind. This is linked to sexual selection: an aspect of natural selection by which some individuals have advantages over others of the same sex in how likely they are to reproduce. These ideas have been applied to humans in order to explain aspects of social behaviour.

> A good start. Now that terms have been identified, the candidate can go on to refer to them in the rest of the essay without having to stop and explain.

Altruistic, or helping at apparent cost to oneself, is one aspect of human social behaviour that can be explained by evolutionary psychology. Reinterpretations of Darwin's original ideas have led us to think in terms of survival of genes rather then survival of individuals. We are driven to preserve our own genes and to preserve individuals who share them. Our children, for example, have 50% of their genes from each parent, and brothers and sisters also share 50% of their genes. Helping related individuals improves their fitness and their ability to pass on our genes. Including related others in our attempts to survive and reproduce leads to 'inclusive fitness' which is measured by the number of our genes represented in the population in ourselves or others.

The effects of inclusive fitness have been tested in studies which present people with hypothetical dilemmas involving saving lives or doing favours. Burnstein *et al.* showed that people would be more likely to save close kin in life or death scenarios and that the health and youth of the person to be saved also played a part. *For ethical reasons these studies cannot involve real emergencies, so although the results support the idea of inclusive fitness it is rare in real life to face such clear-cut choice. Work done in the field observing how people behave in real-life emergencies would have greater ecological validity but this raises problems of control. Talking to people afterwards may be the only option but, by then, they have had time to reflect on what they did and justify their actions in other ways.* Inclusive fitness is also supported by the finding that step-parents are more likely than natural parents to abuse their step-children. People in closeknit societies are more helpful to each other than are those in larger groups.

> A good mix of referenced support for inclusive fitness here, along with some methodological evaluation. The penultimate sentence raises another important issue which could be expanded. Evolutionary theory might explain abuse by the step-parent as an attempt by the abuser to improve their own inclusive fitness at the expense of someone else's. However, the finding referred to could also be explained by a variety of other variables such as poverty and family size. Regarding the closeness of individuals in communities, there are cases where people risk themselves to help unrelated individuals. This is hard to explain unless we regard it as an evolutionary leftover from times when humans typically lived in closeknit groups.

Inclusive fitness cannot explain cases where individuals help unrelated individuals, not knowing whether the favour will be returned. Trivers thinks this would only occur when the costs of helping are small but the benefits of a returned favour could be high. He also thinks a parallel ability to detect cheats who don't repay favours should have evolved, otherwise cheats would prosper and their genes become more frequent in the population. Altruism can help fitness if it is reciprocated and many societies seem to have a norm of reciprocity which helps to safeguard this.

> Good use of the problem of reciprocal altruism here to evaluate the inclusive fitness explanation although the account is theoretical and would benefit from empirical support. A mention of how reciprocal altruism relates to competition and cooperation would also be worthwhile.

The evolutionary approach can also be used to explain how sexual selection in humans has led to different kinds of reproductive behaviour in males and females. Trivers thought that sexual selection came down to male competition and female choice and that these resulted from the different amounts of parental investment made by the two sexes. Human females invest a great deal in producing a small number of offspring so they must choose a male of superior fitness to ensure their efforts are not wasted. Males, on the other hand, could father many offspring at relatively less cost but they must compete with other males and with female choice. Those who compete more successfully have more offspring but if both parents are necessary for the survival of the offspring, males and females tend to invest equally in parenting.

Trivers thinks that males would normally seek many sexual partners to mother their young (polygyny) but are influenced by female choice and the need for parental investment. For example, in impoverished societies, where the young are at risk, polyandry (many husbands for one female) may occur. Symons and Ellis tested these ideas by asking male and female undergraduates whether they would have sexual intercourse with an attractive total stranger if there were no risks involved. Males were four times more likely than females to say that they would. *Although this could be taken as support for Trivers' ideas there are many problems with drawing conclusions from research conducted in this way. Also there is no way of knowing whether what people say they would do corresponds with what they would actually do.*

> There is a great deal to say about many aspects of human reproductive behaviour from an evolutionary point of view. Care must be taken that it does not become speculative and anecdotal.

In conclusion, evolutionary explanations have been criticized for underplaying the role of social and cultural forces in determining human behaviour, seeing humans as over-determined by their biology and ancestry. The danger in this is that people will cease to take responsibility for their actions, arguing that they are victims of their biological nature. There are many exceptions to the predictions made by evolutionary theory which need to be explained, perhaps by other approaches. Nevertheless, taken along with other approaches, evolutionary psychology could help to give a more complete understanding of human behaviour.

> This is quite a well-structured essay which begins well and goes on to address the question's requirements. The choice of apparent altruism as the first aspect of behaviour is a good one and is used well. For the second example, perhaps a specific aspect of human reproductive behaviour could have been chosen and treated in depth, for example, competition between males or the incidence of polygyny, polyandry or monogamy in human societies. Given that knowledge and understanding is well demonstrated on the whole and evaluative skills are evident but need to be elaborated, this essay would probably score about 17 out of 24.

Solutions
Bio-psychology

SOLUTIONS TO REVISION ACTIVITY

See Brain map on page 74.

ESSAY QUESTION AND MARKED SAMPLE ANSWER

Describe and evaluate **two** theories of sleep. *(24 marks)*

> *Examiner's note:* The Skill A and Skill B terms are clearly identified here and are equally weighted. You should divide your time into four allowing ten minutes for each description and ten for each evaluation. The most likely choices are restoration theory and evolutionary theory. You could also make a case that we sleep in order to dream. If you take this route, be sure to focus on one theory (e.g. Freudian psychoanalytic theory). Justify your tactics carefully and explicitly to the examiner and keep the question firmly in mind.

The restoration theory of sleep put forward by Oswald states that sleep gives the body a chance to restore and repair itself both physiologically and psychologically. In a typical night we move through a series of sleep cycles and something different happens in each one. In each cycle there are up to five stages. To test the theory, it is necessary to deprive subjects of different stages of sleep and observe the effects of this. *It should be possible to show the process of repair going on while we sleep is halted if this theory is to be supported.*

Stage five, or REM sleep, is sometimes called active sleep. If sleepers are woken every time they enter REM sleep they show REM rebound when they are allowed to sleep normally as if they are making up for lost time. This means they spent more time in REM and reported more dreaming. Dement, who did some of these studies, at first claimed that loss of REM sleep led to psychotic symptoms *but he later admitted that he had exaggerated the effects. A problem with these studies is that each time a person goes back to sleep they enter REM more quickly and so are woken more often. The effects that are seen are probably caused more by overall sleep loss than by loss of REM itself. Although people recover quickly from REM loss, they do not seem to be able to manage without it completely. This may be because the dreaming that happens in REM sleep has an important function.*

> Good section. The final sentence invites a brief discussion of the function of dreaming and its possible role in both psychological and physiological restoration. It is also worth noting that, although dreaming is closely associated with REM sleep, it also happens in other types of sleep. That it appears to occur less in NREM stages may be due to the fact that people find it more difficult to recall dreams from these. The fact that infants spend so much time in REM suggests that it is associated with neural growth and some research has shown that the rate of protein synthesis is at its highest during REM sleep.

Deprivation of stage four sleep, which is the phase when we sleep most deeply and quietly, seems to lead to physical tiredness and lethargy. But it cannot be shown that this is the only stage when repairs go on, as the body is constantly repairing itself.

> It is worth mentioning here that disturbance in stage four sleep is found in fibrositis sufferers and people deliberately deprived of stage four sleep show similar symptoms to those of fibrositis. Empson (1989) thinks that this provides good evidence that bodily growth and repair happen in stage four sleep while brain growth and repair are dealt with during REM sleep.

Another way to test the theory is to see what happens after exercise. Horne and Minard gave subjects many exhausting activities to do and observed the effects. Physically tired subjects fell asleep more quickly but did not need to sleep for longer.

There are some extreme cases where people have gone without sleep for long periods of time, either as a stunt or because of a disorder. The DJ Peter Tripp stayed awake and on air for 200 hours. At the end of it he was suffering from paranoid delusions and could not do simple mental tasks. His EEG showed the wave pattern of deep sleep even though he was awake. At the end of the study he slept for thirteen hours and all his symptoms disappeared. In an attempt to get into the *Guinness Book of Records*, Randy Gardner stayed awake for 264 hours and suffered no ill effects. Jouvet designed an experiment which preventing cats from sleeping. They were placed on a small platform over water and couldn't relax into REM sleep in case they fell in (the 'flower pot technique'). Jouvet observed that some animals developed hypersexuality and even died. *This evidence is contaminated by the possibility that the animals died from the stress of the situation rather than from lack of sleep.*

> This section is relevant but largely descriptive. More could be made of the fact that studies of extreme sleep-deprivation studies produce mixed results. Peter Tripp was carrying out a stressful job during his period of deprivation, whereas Randy Gardner was able to relax. It is also worth making the point that studies of animals may not transfer easily to humans.

Evolutionary theory is my second theory of sleep. This theory says that the need to sleep has evolved because it helps animals to survive for longer and improves their chances of reproducing. Sleep protects animals from danger. It keeps them out of sight of predators for periods of time, especially at night when animals other than nocturnal ones do not have good vision and they would be more vulnerable than during the day. Another survival function of sleep is that it allows the animal to conserve energy when it needs to, for example, sleeping at night when it is colder reduces their need to generate heat. Desert-dwelling animals may be less active in the day when the heat would be too great for them to conserve enough water. Some animals take this to an extreme and hibernate for long periods of time.

To test this theory it is necessary to compare different species of animal to see if there are any predictable differences in their sleeping patterns. Animals that have to search for food continually should sleep very little. This is true for grazing animals such as cattle. Other animals, such as the big cats, eat infrequently and rest or sleep a great deal. *It should also be the case that animals that are preyed upon by others should sleep less than predators. There is some support for this idea but there are exceptions, and in connection with food searching, that call evolutionary theory into question. Sleep patterns must have evolved because they increased the animal's chances of survival but exceptions to the rules suggest sleep has other important functions as well as improving survival. For example, why should foetuses show active (REM) sleep when they have no way of ensuring their own survival? The theory is also not very readily applied to humans who, if anything, are more likely to be predators than prey.*

There are a number of useful ideas in this section which need to be carefully teased out and examined. For example, the evolution of REM sleep in animals and the pattern of development it shows in human foetuses could be revealing. Mammals also show more REM than reptiles who show none and birds who show very little. This might suggest that it is characteristic of more highly developed brains but, between mammals, there are no predictable patterns. Empson has called the evolutionary theory of sleep a 'waste of time' theory. He thinks that the universality of sleep among animals demonstrates that it must have a more important function than just passing time. It is worth mentioning that a key problem with the theory is its unfalsifiability.

The chances are that sleep performs several useful functions and that there is some truth in all theories.

The candidate has done well to address the requirements of the question and presented a well-organized account with a good attempt to balance Skills A and B. The description of restoration theory lacks detail but the evaluative evidence provided for it fares rather better. The description of evolutionary theory is clear but the evaluation is rather speculative and needs to be supported with some evidence. 15 marks out of 24. (Skill A, 9 marks: bottom of Band 3; Skill B, 6 marks: bottom of Band 2.)

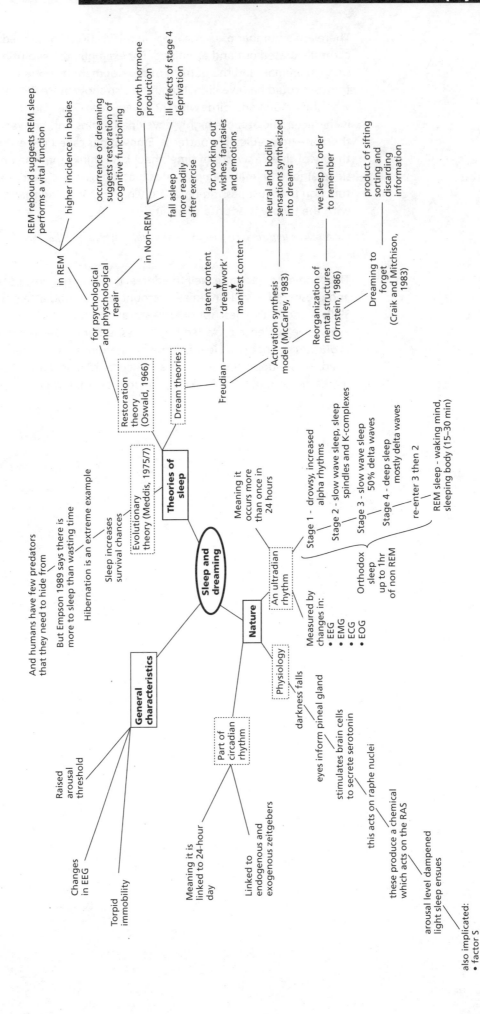

Figure 9: Sleep and dreaming: completed brain map.

4 Solutions
Abnormal psychology

SOLUTIONS TO REVISION ACTIVITY

See Table 13 on page 77.

ESSAY QUESTION AND MARKED SAMPLE ANSWER

Describe and evaluate some of the ways in which psychologists have defined abnormality. *(24 marks)*
(AEB Paper 2, 1992, adapted for new mark scheme)

> *Examiner's note:* The Skill A injunction is 'describe' and the Skill B injunction is 'evaluate' so you must ensure that the approach you take to answering this question allows you scope to do both.

It can be very difficult to decide when a person has a mental disorder and needs help. There is a very thin dividing line between normal and abnormal. Four major approaches have been taken and each of these will be described and evaluated in turn.

Statistically speaking, behaviour is normal if it is what most people show. Abnormal is defined as anything that is atypical, unusual or rare. For all behaviour, this presupposes that there is a range that is considered normal and outside this range, it is abnormal. *There are a number of problems with this model. For one thing, it must be possible to measure the behaviour in question and decide where to cut off normal from abnormal. For another, it takes no account of cultural differences i.e. behaviours occurring frequently in one culture may be considered normal but because they are rare in another they are considered to be abnormal. Another problem is that it does not say what is rare but desirable (e.g. prodigious musical talent) as opposed to undesirable. Undesirable behaviour which is seen as abnormal could also become normal if it occurs frequently enough. Work stress is one example.*

One way round this is to see abnormality as 'deviation from the norm' by which we mean that normal is generally tolerated and accepted behaviour. The norms, however, will usually be decided by the dominant group in society and could be seen as a way of controlling others.

Although these criteria do have weaknesses, they are still widely used and there are some diagnostic tests for measuring rarity (e.g. Eysenck's EPQ).

A strong and information-packed opening section with plenty of Skill B.

Humanistic psychologists, such as Maslow, have offered another approach: that of 'ideal mental health'. Such approaches emphasize the desirability of attaining a goal, such as self-actualization, reached by moving up a hierarchy of needs. Deviations from the ideal are therefore abnormal. Other ideals might be competence in various areas of life or the ability to cope with stress. *Unfortunately, these ideals are often reached by so few that most of us qualify as abnormal. Generally, this approach is weakened by the vagueness of stating and assessing what is ideal.*

Another approach is to see abnormality as something defined by a culture (cultural relativity). Conversely it could be seen as universal and the same in all cultures. *In this latter view, it should be possible to show that the symptoms, progress and response to the treatment of problems is the same anywhere. Cultural relativity would mean that symptoms are expressed differently according to culture. Certainly, it could be that some cultures are more reserved and others 'act out' their symptoms more. Furthermore, as stated earlier, cultures differ in what they consider to be abnormal or normal.*

Again, a good balance of explanation and commentary.

Although the three criteria so far described are important, anyone who refers themselves to a GP for help can expect to be assessed on a variety of practical criteria. The GP might look for evidence of 'suffering' (this could be overt or implied), 'inefficiency' in being able to deal with everyday life or work, 'maladaptiveness' or 'bizarreness' of behaviour. These would be considered along with the symptoms themselves. *How these are judged might shift with the culture or time in which they occur.*

A useful linking paragraph and an astute comment at the end.

If there does seem to be a problem, what happens next depends on who the GP refers the case to and which model of abnormality the professional adopts. The medical approach tends to see problems as diseases affecting the nervous system and brain and may use diagnostic systems to define and label a set of symptoms. *The practical and ethical problems of this are important because they direct treatment and invite labelling. According to Szasz, many disorders are not diseases but problems in living and should be dealt with as such. An important issue is that, when psychiatrists define abnormality, their decision depends a lot on how a person describes their symptoms and this may not be the same for two different people with essentially the same problem. Szasz says this might lead certain people more than others to be 'stigmatized' and excluded. More recently, however, Fonagy and Higgitt (1984) have argued that the use of operational criteria (such as checklists of symptoms) for definition reduce the risk of subjective judgement although it could never be completely eradicated. In defence of the medical approach to defining abnormality, Spitzer (1976) remarked that the unreliability of diagnosis does not mean it is of no value.*

It is difficult to deal effectively with all the issues raised by defining a disorder as a disease, but the candidate manages well in the time available and shows an awareness of the wider consequences of definition.

This is a well-organized and informed essay with a heavy emphasis on Skill B. In the early stages some illustrative examples would have helped to support many of the points made. A mention of models in addition to the medical one would have rounded off the essay nicely. For Skill A a Band 2 mark of 6 is likely and for Skill B a Band 3 mark of 11 gives an overall mark of 17 out of 24.

Table 13: Models of abnormality

Models	Basic assumptions/terms	Treatments and therapies	Comments
Medical (sometimes called biomedical or somatic)	2 Disorders are biogenic 4 Disorders result from infection, neurochemical factors, trauma, inherited systemic defects 13 Disease model	9 ECT 17 Psychopharmacology (including anxiolytics, anti-depressants, antipsychotics) 19 Psychosurgery (rarely)	3 *Firm basis in scientific research 10 Fosters helplessness and passivity 14 Major successes with more serious disorders 19 Symptom relief only? 22 Underplays sociocultural factors 24 Uses classification systems
Behavioural Pavlov, Skinner, Bandura	9 Disorders result from learning maladaptive behaviour patterns 10 Environmental determinism 12 Reinforcement, punishment and extinction 16 Normal and abnormal behaviours are learned via conditioning and modelling 18 The symptoms are all there is to a problem	4 Aversion therapy 5 Can be combined with cognitive approaches 11 Flooding and implosion 12 Behaviour shaping 18 Biofeedback 20 Systematic desensitization 23 Token economies	3 *Firm basis in scientific research 7 Can explain the 'neurotic paradox' 9 Especially good on anxiety disorders 16 Parsimonious 17 Reductionist 20 Tendency to ignore inner person 23 Use of animals in research
Cognitive Beck	8 Disorders result from faulty cognitions 14 Faulty cognitions include irrational or upsetting thoughts, distortions of reality, maladaptive assumptions	1 *Client is responsible for own progress 3 All approaches incorporate uncovering and restructuring cognitive processes 6 Client and therapist work as a team 10 Ellis' rational emotive therapy 15 Meichenbaum's stress-inoculation training	1 *Clients need to be verbally competent 5 Can be rapidly effective on less severe disorders 8 Combines well with behaviourist approaches 18 Scientific backing in cognitive tradition but still involves unobservable processes
Humanistic Rogers, Maslow	1 Emphasizes personal agency, individual freedom, basic goodness 6 Blocks include failure to meet conditions of worth and gulf between ideal self and self-concept 15 Blocks to personal growth and self-actualization cause problems	1 *Client is responsible for own progress 2 A phenomenological approach is taken 13 Includes client-centred therapy (non-directive therapy) and group therapies 21 Therapies are enabling and facilitating 22 Therapists must show warmth, empathy, genuine-ness and unconditional positive regard	1 *Clients need to be verbally competent 2 *Cultural bias 4 *Not effective on more serious psychotic disorders 11 Has contributed to better understanding of therapeutic relationships 12 Lack of coherent theory makes testing difficult 15 Optimistic and intuitively appealing 21 Tends to reject experimental approaches
Psychodynamic Freud (psychoanalytic approach)	3 Disorders stem mainly from neurotic anxiety 5 Behaviour is symptomatic of an underlying problem 7 Role of unconscious is central 11 Fixations and ego defences can cause problems 17 Emphasizes role of early experience	7 Client must become aware of unconscious conflicts 8 Dream analysis, free-association, parapraxes 14 Involves transference, inter-pretation, resistance, working through, catharsis and insight 16 Psychoanalysis	1 *Clients need to be verbally competent 2 *Cultural bias 4 *Not effective on more serious psychotic disorders 6 Can be very time- and money-consuming 13 Lack of scientific backing 25 Weeds out the cause of a problem

5 Solutions
Cognitive psychology

★ SOLUTIONS TO REVISION ACTIVITIES

Revision activity 1 Memorizing the models

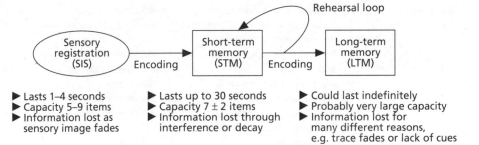

Figure 10: Atkinson and Shiffrin's Two Process Model of Memory.

▶ Lasts 1–4 seconds
▶ Capacity 5–9 items
▶ Information lost as sensory image fades

▶ Lasts up to 30 seconds
▶ Capacity 7 ± 2 items
▶ Information lost through interference or decay

▶ Could last indefinitely
▶ Probably very large capacity
▶ Information lost for many different reasons, e.g. trace fades or lack of cues

Figure 11: Baddeley's Working Memory Model.

Levels of processing

In 1972, Craik and Lockhart proposed that memory depends on how we process incoming information. There are two levels, **shallow** and **deep**. The first of these takes two forms, **structural** and **phonemic** processing. Both of these involve **maintenance** rehearsal and lead to **short-term** retention. The second involves **semantic** processing, **elaborative** rehearsal and **longer term** retention.

Table 14: Bartlett's constructivist memory model

Change	Explanation
Omissions	Certain details are left out in order to make the story flow better.
Rationalizations	Details may be added to make a 'better' account.
Alteration in importance	Aspects of an account may be played up or down.
Changed order	This may make an account flow better.
Added effect	If a person had reacted emotionally to a story, this can affect the nature of the details recalled.

Revision activity 2   Memory aids and memory models

Memory aid	Example	Background theory
Hook or peg system	'One is bun, two is shoe'...	This combines mental imagery with a cue system, so it fits with the two-process model and the work of Paivio.
Method of loci	Remembering who was at a party by talking a 'mental walk' around the party venue.	Paivio again. If the party venue is a familiar place, it may also have personal relevance (Rogers *et al.*)
Rhymes, phrases and stories	Richard of York gave Battle In Vain (for the colours of the rainbow).	Another cue system.
Brain maps	See the example on animal research in Part III, Chapter 8.	These combine chunking, organization, (two-process model) and deep processing (levels model). The use of colour adds distinctiveness (Eysenck).
Preview, question, read, summarize (PQRS)	Studying from a textbook.	Encourages deep processing (levels model).
Re-check original sources	Re-reading an original account to guard against inaccuracies.	Discourages 'effort after meaning', so fits with Bartlett's constructivist model.

ESSAY QUESTION AND MARKED SAMPLE ANSWER

Describe and evaluate research findings into **two** applications of memory research (e.g. eye-witness testimony, memory for medical information). *(24 marks)*

> Examiner's note: The Skill A and B injunctions are obvious here.
> The examiner has suggested examples for you to consider but the wording of the question does not oblige you to use them. You could legitimately choose other areas such as revision techniques or face recognition.
> You should make your choice explicit and ensure that the areas you use really do constitute **two** applications.

Accuracy in eye-witness testimony (EWT) is vital if the police are to do their job properly and wrongful convictions are to be avoided. The study of how the memory works, and how forgetting occurs can help them to understand the ways in which EWT may be unreliable. The memory is like a database. There are three processes involved in memory. These are encoding, storage and retrieval. Information must go through all these stages if it is to be recalled and forgetting can occur at any one of them. *It has been claimed that human memory is so fragile and fallible that it is never to be completely trusted.*

> This is commentary but the second half of this opening paragraph is something of an indulgence if you are writing to a strict time limit. The

> last sentence is rather unsubstantiated. It would be better to get straight to the point and say which two applications are to be used immediately after the first sentence.

In early research, Ebbinghaus used himself as a subject. He learned lists of nonsense syllables and recalled them at intervals over a month. He found that forgetting was rapid at first and then became slower. If he used different materials, and recognition rather then recall, forgetting was less rapid. Apart from showing the superiority of recognition over recall, *Ebbinghaus's methods did not tell us much about memory in everyday life. It was left to others to do that.*

> The relevance of this paragraph really needs to be spelt out.

Bartlett (1932) used completely different methods: repeated reproduction and serial reproduction. In repeated reproduction, a story, picture or passage was presented to a subject who was asked to recall it a day, weeks or even years later. Bartlett found that, if the reproductions were frequent, the recall was a lot more accurate than when it was less frequent. In serial reproduction, a story is presented to one person who tells it to another who tells it to a third and so on until six or seven reproductions have occurred. One such story was *The War of the Ghosts*. Bartlett found that subjects tend to shorten and adapt the story to make it seem more logical, coherent and sensible. This often involved making inferences and these could be influenced by a person's cultural background. When the story is reconstructed by the individual, the distortions include omissions of detail, rationalizations of storylines, added affect, changes in order of information and alterations in the importance of certain events. *This 'tidying up' of the story is an idea strongly supported by Gestalt theorists.*

> OK, but the relevance of this material to EWT could be made much clearer early on in the paragraph.

This view that memory is reconstructive in nature is also taken by Elizabeth Loftus who argues that this is one reason why EWT can be so unreliable. She claimed that the type of reconstruction made by someone could be distorted by the kinds of questions with which their memories were prompted. In a laboratory setting she showed two groups of students' films of a car accident. Later on, she asked the first group: 'Did you see *the* broken headlight?' The second group were asked: 'Did you see *a* broken headlight?' In fact no broken headlight had appeared in the film. However, 15% of the '*the*' group answered 'yes' compared to 7% of the '*a*' group. Later, Bekerian and Bowers (1983) showed that the effect of leading questions could be reduced if the order of questions followed the order of events in an incident. *Nevertheless, in 1974, Cole and Pringle also claimed that evidence of identification is virtually worthless, thus, now, judges have been required to inform jurors about the possible limitations of EWT.*

> Good level of detail here along with some assessment and commentary.

Contrary to this view, some researchers suggest that subjects will not inevitably be misled by leading questions. In 1986, Yuille and Cutshall showed the volume of accurate detail reproduced by eye-witnesses to a shooting incident was truly impressive under Loftus's leading question technique. Significantly, the wording of the misleading questions had no effect and those most deeply distressed by the incident were the most accurate. *It seems that memory for important information that is accurately perceived at the time is not easily distorted.*

> Assessment appears here i.e. appraising the value of the conclusions.

All these findings show it is important to be aware of the possible effect of leading questions. It is also sensible to gather several EWTs of the same event. Providing subjects do not all distort their accounts in the same way, it should be possible to pick out some agreement to get a more reliable result. Another important idea is that accounts should be gathered as soon as possible after an event and witnesses allowed to practise their recall. Finally, reconstructions of a crime, or events leading up to it, could help to get witnesses to reconstruct their memory of a real crime more accurately.

Interpretation and commentary are well done here.

As well as events, witnesses are often asked to recall faces and this is where face-recognition research comes in. Ebbinghaus showed object recognition is better than recall. Does the same apply for faces? Hochberg and Galper (1967) conducted an experiment using photographs of faces. Subjects were first shown 35 photos and then 60 photos. They were then shown fifteen pairs of photographs. One photo from each pair had been shown previously. The recognition of the photo previously shown was better for the 35 photo condition but there was still 90% recognition level for the 60 photos. In 1969, Yin observed 96% correct recognition of male faces presented as photos.

The structure of the essay could be clarified by providing a 'signpost' e.g. 'The second application of memory research to be discussed concerns an area closely related to EWT: that of face recognition.' Some good use of research, however.

This is a high level of accuracy but, because it is laboratory based, it does not say much about real-life face recognition. In such studies, subjects may be aware that they will be asked if they can recognize the faces later on. They therefore give each face their full attention for a time, which might not be how they would normally behave. In further studies, Cross et al. (1971) found that females were significantly better in their testimonies when observing a female face *but this may not hold in real-life situations.* Bahrick et al. (1975) found that in stress-free situations, females are superior in their recognition and recall of people after interactions. Males, though, have better recall and recognition of people after stressful situations. *This may have some bearing on the accuracy of EWT after violent incidents or crimes.*

Good, thoughtful mixture of Skills A and B here.

Face recognition in general is not very efficient. Davies et al. *(1981) showed that people found making photofits, even of familiar individuals, very difficult to do. Given that criminals also often disguise themselves and the witness is unlikely to see their faces for long, photofits must be very inaccurate.* In a real-life setting, Bahrick et al. (1975) tested people's memory for names and faces of former schoolmates over up to 50 years. Memory was tested in a number of ways, sometimes for names alone, sometimes for faces alone and sometimes for fitting names to faces. Recall for all of these dropped over a period of 50 years, especially at the end of this period, perhaps because people were much older by then. Recognition remained high in all conditions. *One confounding variable that could not be controlled in this study was that many of the schoolmates had grown older together and had not lost touch. A better test would be to look at recall or recognition in people who had been to school together and then lost touch.*

Once again Skills A and B are effectively mixed.

This is an impressive essay, given the constraints of examination conditions. It is relevant and well-detailed and the candidate has achieved a good balance of Skills A and B. The structure could have been made a little clearer, perhaps by getting to the point of the essay sooner and by clarifying the two applications to be used. The section on EWT has some theoretical background but the section on face recognition does not. For this reason a bottom Band 3 mark would be likely (10 marks). The Skill B is generally well done, although it could be developed further (bottom of Band 3, 9 marks). The total mark for this essay would be in the region of 19 out of 24.

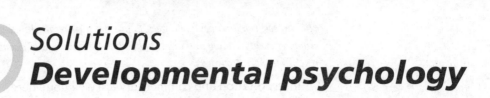

Solutions
Developmental psychology

SOLUTION TO REVISION ACTIVITY

Revision activity   Brainstorm on moral development

1   Punishment tends to have negative effects on the relationship between the punisher and the punished person. On its own it does not teach alternative ways of responding. It models to the punished person a coercive way of getting what you want from others.

2   Research has shown that children pay more attention to what people do than to what they say. As a result they are more likely to imitate expressed behaviour than expressed opinions. If parents want children to absorb their standards they should show consistency in their own opinions and behaviour.

3   The first part of the superego is the ego-ideal which gives us feelings of worth if we do well. The second part is the conscience which makes us feel guilty if we behave badly.

4   Heteronomous morality means that moral behaviour is controlled by forces outside the individual. Autonomous morality refers to moral behaviour that is controlled from within the individual.

5   (a) reciprocal; (b) retributive; (c) rational.

6

LEVEL	I		II		III	
STAGE	1	2	3	4	5	6
STATEMENT	b	a	f	d	e	c

7   Gilligan suggested that Kohlberg's theory is based on masculine values of justice, whereas women tend to concentrate on caring. She was critical of Kohlberg's theory of moral development which she thought was biased towards males since care-oriented reasoning scores lower than justice-oriented reasoning in Kohlberg's scheme.

8   *Social learning theory:*
▶   A parsimonious explanation of moral behaviour.
▶   The theory can explain the inconsistency of moral behaviour across situations.

Freudian theory
▶   No direct evidence for the Oedipal and Electra conflicts because they are unobservable. The problems experienced by Little Hans, which supported the idea of the Oedipal conflict, can be explained in more direct ways than invoking the idea of unconscious mind.
▶   There is no evidence that females are morally weaker than males. If anything, they seem better able to resist temptation.

Piaget's theory
▶   Piaget may have underestimated children's reasoning abilities as a result of presenting moral problems in particularly inaccessible ways.
▶   Nevertheless the general trend of development set out in his theory has been borne out many times by research.

Kohlberg's theory

▶ Cross-cultural studies (e.g. Snarey, 1985) support Kohlberg's claim that his theory is universal. People everywhere follow the same sequence of development but in less-developed rural cultures stage four is usually the highest stage reached compared to modern Western cultures where stage five is usually the highest.

▶ People may reason at higher levels than they behave, so Kohlberg's theory tells us what they think but not what they do.

Gilligan's theory

▶ Bee (1992) says that, in general, studies of sex differences in moral reasoning in children show no differences in the tendency to base judgements on care. In adults, however, women do seem to centre their judgements on care more than do men.

▶ Gilligan has alerted us to a possible bias in the way we think of moral issues: in other words, it is determined by males.

ESSAY QUESTION AND MARKED SAMPLE ANSWER

Discuss the role of social factors in the development of gender. *(24 marks)*

> *Examiner's note:* The injunction discussed requires you to both describe (Skill A) and to evaluate (Skill B). In other words, you should show knowledge and understanding and be able to make an informed judgement about the value of the ideas and the research you describe in your essay. Good selection and organization will earn credit, as will an ability to present an eclectic view.

The first thing to note is the distinction between sex and gender. Sex is our physical status and refers to our biological type as male or female. It can be defined in a number of ways according to external appearance and internal physiological differences. Gender, however, is a psychological or cultural term which denotes whether we are masculine or feminine. Usually sex and gender correspond but there can be inconsistencies, as with hermaphrodites.

Sex is something which cannot be changed but gender is much more flexible. It develops through several stages giving a continuous and persistent sense of ourselves as masculine or feminine. It can be influenced and is not pre-set by sex.

Good scene setting here. It is useful to clarify terms at the outset.

But what factors affect our attitudes and behaviour and indeed the gender that we decide we are? There are a number of theories to explain gender differences. I am going to use Social Learning Theory – SLT (Bandura, 1966).

According to McLoughlin (1971) SLT covers 'behaviour learned in interpersonal situations and linked to the needs that require for their satisfaction the mediation of other people'. SL theorists do not deny the importance of conditioning but they believe that it cannot fully explain the production of novel behaviour. SLT emphasizes observational learning to explain this: learning through watching the behaviour of another person called a 'model'.

Certain characteristics of the model make it more or less likely that the learner will imitate. The conditions under which the model is observed are also important. Learning is spontaneous with no deliberate effort by the learner to learn or the teacher to teach. There is no reinforcement: exposure to the model is all that is needed. But imitation depends, among other things, on the consequences of behaviour for the model. It is possible to learn both very specific behaviour like mannerisms and very general behaviour from models, for example, a sex role.

Observational learning will take place if the following cognitive factors are present: the learner must pay attention, be able to encode what they see, remember the behaviour, be capable of reproducing it and have some motivation to reproduce it.

Bandura found that boys were more likely to imitate aggressive male models than were girls. But how representative are these findings? Are children more likely to imitate same-sex models? *Evidence is mixed. Some investigations have found it to be true and others false. Some SL theorists have not found sufficient evidence to show that children prefer same-sex models. They seem to observe both sexes equally. It may be that their imitation depends on whether they see the behaviour of the model reinforced.*

> **A good attempt to provide theoretical background here, eventually bringing the essay round to the specific problem of sex and gender.**

Parents are the most likely sex-role models children will be exposed to but they are also exposed to peers and many models in the mass media, especially television. There is a great deal of evidence to suggest that the media present the sexes in very stereotyped ways. In 1987, audience research showed that 4–7-year-olds watch an average of 2.8 hours of television a day. The content of this is traditional and stereotyped in the way it presents the sexes. *This avid consumerism is likely to have some effect on the child.*

> **An opportunity has been missed here to explore the role of parents and peers in shaping and modelling sex-role behaviour.**

A study by Gunter (1986) showed that children classed as heavy viewers of television had much more stereotypical views of the sexes than light viewers. *This can be used as evidence in favour of SLT although the specific nature of what children watched does not seem to have been determined.* Further studies have analysed the content of advertisements. Harris and Stobart (1986) found strong evidence of sex-role stereotyping in their study. *This is important because adverts are especially designed to grab attention and be memorable.*

> **The link between media portrayal of the sexes and the viewer's behaviour needs to be questioned here. The research so far described does not do this. Expressed attitudes are not always linked to behaviour.**

In conclusion it seems that gender is influenced by biological factors but also by social ones. The similarities between the sexes are far greater than the differences but in our society we persist in making strong distinctions between the sexes. This suggests that gender is much more a social than a biological matter.

> **This is a thoughtful conclusion but it is not adequately supported by the evidence presented in the essay.**

> **This essay starts well with a strong emphasis on theory. However, the early promise is not fulfilled. The candidate needed to explain clearly what predictions can be made from SLT and how these have been translated into research studies. These could then be evaluated. Conditioning theory could have been treated much more thoroughly in this respect. There are also many different kinds of models from which an individual might learn. The candidate mentions parents, peers and the mass media but concentrates only on the latter. Cultural factors are also very important and deserve to be discussed more fully. Alternative approaches could have been introduced to help the evaluation, such as psychodynamic and cognitive developmental theories, which have plenty to offer and are a good balance to theories with a social emphasis. On the whole the essay contains relevant and well-organized material but it is noticeably light on Skill B. A mark of 12 out of 24 is likely.**

Solutions
Theoretical perspectives and philosophical issues

Revision activity 1   The humanistic approach

Humanistic psychology is sometimes referred to as the 'third force' in psychology (after psychoanalysis and behavourism). A number of theories qualify as being humanistic: two of the most well-known are those of Rogers (1902–1987) and Maslow (1908–1970). As the name suggests, humanistic psychologists focus on the subjective experience of living rather than empirically observable behaviour. It is often said that this was a backlash against the behavourist emphasis on scientific method which was seen as losing sight of the human being.

Basic assumptions

▶ Humanistic psychologists emphasize the study of the whole person rather than reducing behaviour to S–R units or responses to instinctive forces.

▶ They say the focus of study should be on conscious awareness.

▶ People are seen as freely exercising choice over how to behave. They are the architects of their own lives and 'personal agents' in their own psychological growth. These things lead to their uniqueness.

▶ People are basically good.

▶ People are motivated to strive for personal growth and to self-actualize (achieve their potential).

▶ Scientific method is largely inappropriate for studying human experience or, at least, it does not go far enough.

Methods

▶ Subjective self-report is central to understanding human experience. Only the individual knows what their personal experience and behaviour means so they are the best source of information on these matters.

▶ Consciousness has many levels, so studies of altered states of consciousness are revealing. Some humanistic psychologists have studied such things as hypnotic trances, drug-induced states, meditative states, the effects of sensory deprivation or flooding and 'peak experiences'.

Contributions

▶ Humanistic psychologists gave us a new, global model of human behaviour that was refreshingly different from the dominant determinist approaches.

▶ Rogers developed 'client-centred therapy': an approach to psychological problems based on humanistic principles. This therapy put the client and 'facilitator' on a more equal footing and empowered the individual to find their own solutions to their problems. Many other useful humanistic therapies exist.

▶ Client-centred therapy has led to the closer examination of factors in successful psychotherapy, such as an atmosphere of genuineness, warmth, empathy and unconditional positive regard created by the facilitator.

► Humanistic techniques have wide applications in other areas of human functioning, such as in the workplace, in relationships and in education. It has helped us to a better understanding of such diverse things as how people experience joy or face death.

Comments

► The degree to which we can have 'personal agency' may have been over-emphasized. People may be more constrained in life than humanistic psychologists suggest.
► The lack of a coherent theory to work from has made the testing of humanistic ideas difficult (although Rogers did make progress towards testing the progress of client-centred therapy).
► Some of the ideas, such as self-actualization and the requirements for personal growth, are not well-defined, so it is not always possible to demonstrate whether they are occurring.
► The emphasis on the uniqueness of the individual may be biased towards the individualism which characterizes Western culture. Consequently, the theory may not be applicable in other cultures.

Revision activity 1   The cognitive approach

In contrast to the psychoanalytic approach, which emphasizes the role of the unconscious, and the behavourist approach, which emphasizes observable behaviour, the cognitive approach focuses on how we internally process information in the so-called 'black box' of the mind. Cognitive psychology is very broad. It incorporates many fields of research which are all united in their aim to study the ways in which we deal with information from the world and come to understand it.

Basic assumptions

► Behaviour cannot be fully understood without recourse to the internal mental processes, or mediators, that occur between input and output.
► Human functioning can be likened to that of a machine which selects and accepts input from the senses, organizes it and processes it through a number of stages before the output, or cognition, is produced.
► The nature of the information-processing system seems to be inborn. This suggests that all our behaviour is ultimately determined by the nature of the system although there may be some room for choice and decision.
► The way the information-processing system works suggests that human behaviour is rational and predictable. Combined with the determinism assumed in the previous point, this opens cognitive psychology to the scientific method.

Methods

These depend on the branch of cognitive psychology concerned, for example:

► Traditional cognitive psychology uses laboratory-based methods familiar in well-known information-processing studies of memory, attention or perception (e.g. Broadbent's dichotic listening tasks or memory-span procedures).
► With relatively recent advances in computer technology, the newer 'cognitive science' can concentrate on programming computers to mimic, or simulate, the workings of the human brain. Some research in this area has begun by asking people to verbalize their thought processes as they tackle a task. This 'verbal protocol' can be analysed for patterns which help in designing computer simulations.
► Cognitive neuropsychologists compare cognition in brain-damaged individuals

and intact individuals, for example, the famous case of H. M. who has been studied by many psychologists interested in how memory works.

▶ Cognitive developmentalists, such as Piaget, have studied thought processes by examining children's verbal responses to logical problems. Some cognitive psychologists research into eye-witness memory by comparing people's verbal accounts of an event with the actual event.

Contributions

▶ Many different cognitive processes, such as memory, language comprehension and production, problem-solving, attention and perception are more fully understood because of cognitive psychology research.

▶ This research has many practical uses, such as in training air-traffic controllers, designing human operated machinery, devising instructions or improving memory.

▶ Cognitive psychology has been incorporated into a number of other areas of psychology to good effect, for example, in cognitive development research, in cognitive behavioural techniques in clinical settings and in social cognition in social psychology research.

Comments

▶ The emphasis on experimental work has led some critics to question the ecological validity of some of the findings. For example, how much can laboratory studies of memory tell us about everyday memory?

▶ The machine reductionism of the cognitive science approach may not ultimately be sufficient to explain the amazing complexity of the functioning of the human brain.

▶ The implication of assuming that we share similar information-processing systems is that we will process information in broadly similar ways. Differences between people might result from past experiences modifying how we process information, otherwise there may be some mechanism for exercising choice. As cognitive psychologists have problems explaining the exact nature of these influences, the approach remains somewhat deterministic.

▶ It is not entirely clear what 'information' is. Some laboratory studies can narrow it down but, in real life, the input we receive is not 'out of context' in this way. Instead it occurs in a social, cultural and historical context which must all affect what we make of it. Language input is a particularly good example.

▶ The focuses of research in cognitive psychology tend to be rather narrow. A fuller understanding of cognition will only be possible if the focuses can be drawn together and their interaction understood.

▶ Some critics would argue that cognitive psychology is simply an extension of behavourism because it attempts to discover what lies between stimuli and responses. This may simply be more strings of stimuli and responses.

Revision activity 1   The biological approach

The aim of biological psychology is twofold: first, to help in the understanding of the role of genetics in behaviour, and second to understand the role of physiology (especially the structure and function of the nervous system) in behaviour. Out of this we shall, hopefully, arrive at a clearer understanding of how nature and nurture interact, since both are important in understanding behaviour.

Basic assumptions

► The basis of behaviour is largely physiological. It can be understood in terms of the structure and function of the nervous system and the endocrine system which produces hormones.
► Both heredity and environment have an important part to play in nervous system structure and function. The interaction of nature and nurture therefore needs to be understood.
► Since human nervous systems are similar in structure, the general principles of functioning can be discovered.
► Behaviour is rational and predictable.

Methods

The methods employed are largely of the kind associated with the scientific method, particularly experimentation. They include:

► Comparative studies of humans and animals can help to throw light on the relationship between nervous system structure and function.
► The effects of drugs (especially psychoactive ones) and their effects on behaviour are often studied. Drugs are, technically, substances foreign to the body that have to be introduced into it in some way.
► Electrical stimulation of the brain (ESB) using small electric currents delivered via tiny electrodes can help us to understand the localization of function in the brain.
► Accidental injury to the brain can help us to understand brain function without the ethical constraints inherent in deliberately damaging the brain.
► Psychosurgery, such as splitting the brain, has been used to study, among other things, the nature of consciousness.
► Electrical recording techniques, such as EEG, are useful for studies relating brain activity to different levels of consciousness.

Contributions

These are very wide-ranging. A selection is offered here:

► The role of genetic factors in behaviour is increasingly well understood, especially the extent to which heredity and environment interact, such as in conditions like schizophrenia.
► The approach has contributed much to our understanding of the physiological basis of many psychological states, such as emotion, motivation and the different levels of awareness.
► Our understanding of the structure and function of the nervous system has many practical applications, for example, in chemotherapy designed to help people cope with a wide range of psychologically manifested problems.
► Research into stress, and the extent to which people can resist its damaging effects, has grown into the new field of psychoimmunology which combines our understanding of how psychological factors combine with the action of the nervous and endocrine systems to affect our immune system.

Comments

► The physiological system is extremely complex and our techniques for studying it are still relatively crude. Advances in biological psychology are therefore largely constrained by the available technology.
► One of the greatest problems for biological psychology is explaining such phenomena as consciousness and the 'mind–body' relationship. Some critics argue that scientific attempts to understand such things are doomed to failure.
► Although nature–nurture questions are being addressed, it is technically impossible to separate one from the other and determine exactly what role they play in determining behaviour.

▶ The biological approach under-emphasizes the role of social and cultural factors which are apparently so influential in human behaviour. There is a good case here for combining several levels of explanation.

Revision activity 2 Theoretical perspectives and philosophical issues

	Perspectives				
Issues	*Psychoanalytic*	*Behaviourist*	*Humanistic*	*Cognitive*	*Biological*
Freedom and determinism	3	1	2	5	4
Reductionism	3	5	4	2	1
Nature and nuture	4	5	1	2	3
Idiographic/ nomothetic	5	4	1	2 or 3	2 or 3
Objectivity/ subjectivity	5	1	4	3	2

Table 18: Revision activity 2: Theoretical perspectives and philosophical issues

Issues	1. Psychoanalytic	2. Behaviourist	3. Humanistic	4. Cognitive	5. Biological
Freedom and determinism	Behaviour is biologically determined by the operation of primarily sexual and aggressive instinctive forces although early experiences also affect how we behave.	Behaviour is mainly environmentally determined through conditioning experiences, although some biological determinism occurs through genetic limitations. (Pigs can't fly!)	Past experiences count but people are generally free to choose how to behave, based on their assessment of a situation. They are responsible for their own behaviour.	Behaviour is 'freely determined': there is some selection and interpretation of stimuli and some decision and choice, but these operate within the constraints of the existing system.	Behaviour is doubly determined (genetically and environmentally). People have no choice over heredity or environment and these factors interact to produce behaviour.
Reductionism	This approach is an example of biological reductionism (seeing instinctive forces as driving behaviour).	An early view in this approach was that behaviour could be reduced to S–R associations. Later views incorporate cognitions.	Reductionism is rejected in favour of 'holism' which advocates the study of the whole human being.	An extreme form of reductionism applied here is machine reductionism where the system is seen to operate on input like a computer.	Reductionism operates on a number of levels. The most basic is to explain behaviour in terms of the structure and function of the nervous system.
Nature and nurture	Innate biological forces (nature) are paramount but early experiences interact with these to shape personality.	Environmental experiences are paramount (nurture) although our physical make-up will impose limitations.	Shared biological type (nature) means that humans are all motivated by the same need to achieve their potential. Life (nurture) can help or hinder this.	Nature and nurture cannot be separated. The organization and operation of the brain and how we process information are affected by both.	Nature and nurture are inseparable. They determine our physical make-up and interact to produce behaviour.
Idiographic/ nomothetic	Idiographic and nomothetic. Individual personalities are based on unique experiences but the course of development is nomothetic (generally applicable to all).	Nomothetic. This approach attempts to discover laws of behaviour which are generally applicable to all.	Idiographic. This approach studies unique individuals, seeing them as architects of their own lives.	Nomothetic. General principles of structure and functioning that apply to everyone are sought.	Nomothetic. General principles of structure and functioning that apply to everyone are sought.
Objectivity/ subjectivity	Subjectivity. This stems mainly from the use of clinical case studies which are used to gather subjective reports. These are then subjectively interpreted.	Objectivity. The adoption of the scientific approach is central to this approach, hence the emphasis on objectivity.	Subjectivity. The individual's subjective experience is more important in understanding behaviour than an outside observer's interpretations.	Objectivity. This springs from the original view of humans as machines whose structure and function can be viewed in an objective, scientific way.	Objectivity. Stemming from the view of humans as biological machines, whose structure and function can be studied objectively to see how they relate to behaviour.

ESSAY QUESTION AND MARKED SAMPLE ANSWER

Discuss contributions of the behaviourist approach to psychology.
(24 marks)

> *Examiner's note:* The injunction 'Discuss' invites both description and evaluation and it can be assumed that there are 12 marks for each. The material that could be used in this essay is vast. A choice will probably be needed between breadth and depth. It would be legitimate, for example, to examine practical applications in a special area such as education, as long as this was clearly justified. Another approach would be to take a much wider view and to talk generally about many areas of psychology touched on by behaviourism.

Behaviourism is said to have begun with J. B. Watson (1913) who felt that Wundt's introspection lacked objectivity and would not help psychology to progress. The mind could not be studied directly, so Watson believed psychologists should concentrate on studying behaviour. He thought it could eventually be reduced to learned S–R units and that psychology should focus on how such learning took place.

> Good scene-setting here. It would help to emphasize that this shift in the focus of psychology could be seen as a contribution. There is also more that could be said about what this contribution entailed in terms of the view of human behaviour as being, for example, environmentally determined and governed by general laws of behaviour.

The main contribution of behaviourism is in explaining learning. Classical conditioning is one kind and was first studied by Pavlov. This type of learning builds on innate reflexes and can explain how we learn fears and emotional reactions. A neutral stimulus occurring close in time to a stimulus that naturally evokes a fear or emotional response soon becomes capable of bringing about the response on its own.

Operant conditioning is another kind of learning for which Skinner is best known. He investigated Thorndike's Law of Effect in detail and concluded that behaviour was determined by its consequences. The investigation of these consequences (reinforcement and punishment) is one of Skinner's greatest contributions. He showed how behaviour such as driving or other skills could be built up through trial and error and by shaping until they were extremely skilled. Behaviour could also be extinguished by altering its consequences.

Social learning theory is another important contribution. It is associated with Bandura and Mischel who used the ideas of reinforcement and punishment to explain how behaviour is learned but added that these consequences in humans are often social ones. Behaviour is also learned from others by observation and imitation. Part of the work of social learning theorists was to take some of Freud's psychoanalytic ideas and explain them in terms of learning theory.

> Quite a good summary. It appears that this candidate is going for breadth, rather than depth, in this essay. This is all Skill A so far.

The learning approach has been applied in many different areas of psychology to explain how learning comes about. In the field of perception, for example, Annis and Frost (1973) studied the effect of the cultural environment on perception in Cree Indians who led either traditional or urban lives. They found that traditional Cree Indians could identify parallel lines in any orientation. Urban Indians could only do this with vertical or horizontal parallel lines.

Behaviourism has also contributed to our understanding of abnormality. It explains how conditions such as phobias could be learned (through classical conditioning) and how they can be treated, for example, through behaviour therapies such as systematic desensitization. Conditions could also be learned through operant conditioning or observation. For example, an agoraphobic's behaviour could be maintained by the attention every feeling of panic brings about. Behaviour-modification programmes changing reinforcement contingencies can help in such cases. Other phobias could be passed on from parents to children through modelling, so observing models showing no fear should help.

> This would be a good place to offer a bit more detail in the form of examples. Some evaluation of the behaviourist approach to abnormality would go well here, for example, in terms of whether its basis in animal research means that it is applicable to humans and whether the therapies really do remove the problem or just the symptom.

As well as many practical applications, behaviourism has made important theoretical contributions. More than any other approach, it has been successful in applying scientific methods to studying behaviour. It can explain a wide range of behaviour in ways that do not call on unobservables such as the unconscious mind. It has been criticized for its basis in animal research, for its environmental determinism and its reductionism. Radical behaviourism cannot explain everything if it insists on using only overt behaviour. At least some of our behaviour is the result of cognitive processes that go on between stimulus and response. Humanistic psychologists argue that behaviourism is missing the point and that psychology should concentrate on studying the nature of human experience instead. Today, few behaviourists would subscribe to the extreme views of the early workers. In treatments, for example, they would mix the best of their own approach with other approaches to achieve the best result for the individual. Used in this way, behaviourism can make a worthwhile contribution.

> Many relevant examples of Skill B here but, as this is the only place it appears, it needs to be expanded. It could include an evaluation of the effectiveness of some of the many applications of behaviourism, for example, and, perhaps, a defence against some of the criticisms made.

> This answer tends to dart about between topics. Nevertheless it is well-organized and nicely rounded off. The variety of material gives it eclecticism but detail tends to be lacking. The candidate does not lose sight of the question, as evidenced by many 'signposts' throughout the essay. For Skill A a bottom of Band 3 mark is likely (10) and for Skill B, a bottom of Band 2 mark (5), making a total of 15 out of 24.

Solutions
Ethics

SOLUTION TO REVISION ACTIVITIES

Revision activity 1 Ethical considerations in Milgram's obedience to authority study (1974)

Outline of study

Ethical guideline (BPS, 1993)	Comment
1 ✓ General	1 Milgram argued that he had considered the ethical implications and psychological consequences of his research for participants but could not know in advance how things would turn out.
2 ✓ Informed consent	2 Not obtained because of deception.
3 ✓ Deception	3 This was an integral part of the research design. Without it, Milgram reasoned, the research would have been pointless.
4 ✓ Debriefing	4 Included post-experimental interviews and questionnaires. The latter were used up to a year afterwards.
5 ✓ Withdrawal	5 Participants were pressed not to withdraw, although Milgram claimed they were free to do so.
6 ✓ Confidentiality and privacy	6 These were properly observed.
7 ✓ Protection of participants	7 A number of participants were extremely upset by the procedures involved. Baumrind argues Milgram did not do enough to protect them from psychological harm.
8 ✗ Observational research	8
9 ✗ Giving advice	9
10 ✓ Monitoring colleagues	10 Milgram 'piloted' his research design by asking 14 psychology students and 40 professors to consider its acceptability.

Concluding comments
Did the ends justify the means? Milgram had to defend his view that the knowledge gained was important and justify the apparently short-term cost to the participants. His debriefing procedures were thorough and the majority of participants (about 98 per cent) either felt neutral or were glad to have taken part. Some felt the gain in awareness of factors involved in obedience had been personally valuable. One way to get over the deception used in this study would be to ask fully informed participants to role-play, although the ecological validity of the research would then be even more arguable (see Zimbardo's' study, next.) Milgram has commented that people's alarm about his study may be more to do with the wider social implications of his findings than with ethical issues.

Revision activity 1   Extra solution: Ethical considerations in Zimbardo *et al.*'s prison-simulation study (1973)

Outline of study

Zimbardo *et al.* recruited 25 young men to take part in a two-week prison-simulation exercise. These volunteers, especially selected for their general health and mental stability, were randomly assigned to role-play prisoners or guards. Within a short time, guards began to exert power and authority over prisoners in, sometimes, very demeaning ways. The prisoners, in turn, became increasingly passive and demoralized. The study was stopped after six days because of the unacceptable levels of distress being experienced by the prisoners.

Ethical guideline (BPS, 1993)		*Comment*	
1	✓ General	1	Zimbardo *et al.* considered the ethical implications and psychological consequences of their research design in advance but were not able to predict how the study would progress.
2	✓ Consent	2	The 25 volunteers gave fully informed consent to take part in the study.
3	✗ Deception	3	
4	✓ Debriefing	4	Full post-study interviews, discussions and debriefings and follow-ups were held with prisoners and guards both independently and together.
5	✓ Withdrawal	5	Volunteers were free to withdraw but prisoners may have felt under pressure from the guards to remain.
6	✓ Confidentiality and privacy	6	Zimbardo *et al.* observed this guideline but some participants chose to reveal their identities through giving talks on their college courses, becoming involved in prison reform or selling their stories to *Life* magazine.
7	✓ Protection of participants	7	Zimbardo *et al.* stopped their study when it became apparent that prisoners' levels of distress were unacceptable.
8	✗ Observational research	8	
9	✗ Giving advice	9	
10	✓ Monitoring colleagues	10	Zimbardo *et al.*'s research design had been carefully considered and approved for funding.

Concluding comments
Zimbardo *et al.* used no deception whatsoever in their study but even role-play led to distress for the participants who played prisoners. Zimbardo was convinced that the participants' suffering was confined to the research situation and that, on balance, they had gained from the experience. The wider implications of the findings were also thought to be important in understanding the effects of prison regimes on prisoners and guards although the study's ecological validity could be in question. As with Milgram's study, alarm about the research methods employed may be, at least in part, a result of discovering unpleasant things of a socially sensitive nature.

Revision activity 2 Psychological research and the use of animals

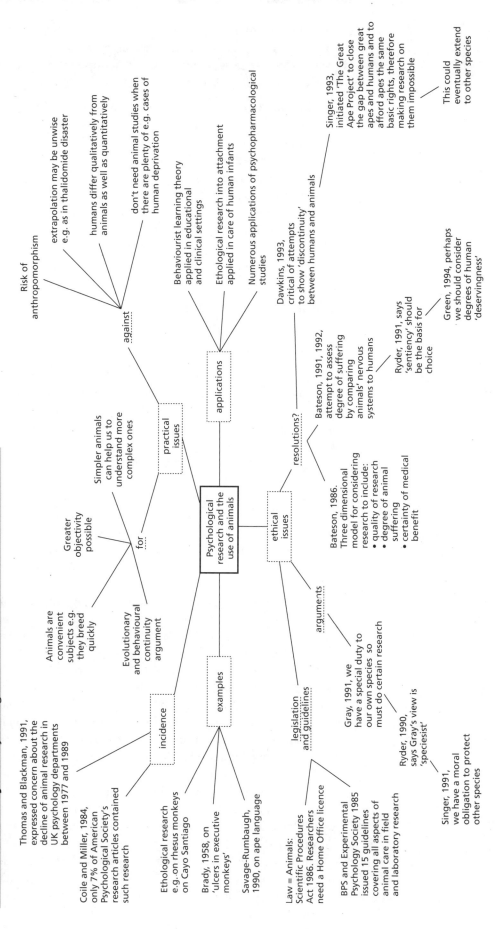

Figure 12: Completed brain map.

1a Outline the main ethical considerations involved in psychological investigations using human participants. *(12 marks)*

1b With reference to two studies, assess attempts made by psychologists to resolve these issues. *(12 marks)*

> *Examiner's note:* The wording of the question is almost the same as on the AEB syllabus so it shouldn't take you by surprise. The Skill A in this question is required in (a) and the Skill B in (b). Part (b) is clearly directing you to use real research examples as opposed to dealing with purely theoretical issues and the 12 marks available will be awarded pro-rata. You are being asked for two mini-essays, so label your answer clearly to show which bit is which. If you do inadvertently include Skill A in part (b) or vice versa, the examiner will still credit it in the appropriate part.

Answer to part (a)

In all aspects of research and practice, psychologists work within a set of ethical guidelines. In research, the BPS guidelines are the ones psychologists should follow. *These are to protect the research participant and researcher as well as the reputation of psychology in the public's opinion.*

Good strong start showing awareness of wider issues.

The first guideline is a general one urging psychologists to take account of all the possible consequences for the research participants, bearing in mind the differences they could have in age, sex, personality and ethnic group. *This can be difficult to do, so pilot studies are to be recommended wherever possible.* The aim of this is to protect the rights and dignity of participants and the reputation of psychology.

The second guideline is about consent but really means 'fully informed consent'. The researcher should explain all aspects of the investigation to participants so that they know what they are agreeing to do. If consent cannot be directly obtained, those representing the participant can sometimes give it for them: for example, parents for children or those taking responsibility for others, such as the carers of intellectually impaired participants. The researcher should not offer inducements to get people to cooperate against their will or do anything more risky than would normally occur in everyday life. *This is an issue in USA universities where students may be required to act as participants as a condition of coming on their course.*

The third guideline is to do with deception by withholding information or deliberately misleading participants. This should be avoided wherever possible although sometimes deception is necessary to make an investigation work. The psychologist must be sure that there is no other way to collect the data before using deception. The fourth guideline concerns debriefing. This must be 'active intervention' so that the researcher works hard to ensure that participants understand all aspects of the research and the findings. If the participant needs help in coming to terms with any aspect of the research, the psychologist is obliged to help and try to return them to the state in which they first entered the research. Intention to debrief is no excuse for deception.

The fifth guideline is that participants must know they have the right to withdraw from the investigation at any point without penalty. Even at the end of the study, participants may request to have the data they provided destroyed. The sixth guideline, confidentiality, comes under the legislation of the Data

Protection Act. It means that participants can expect that their identities will not be revealed unless they give prior consent. Again, this guideline protects both participants and the researcher.

The seventh guideline states that the researcher has a duty to protect participants from physical or psychological harm during the research. Participants can help in this by informing the researcher of anything which might put them at risk, for example, certain medical conditions. The eighth guideline is about observational research and says that the investigator should only observe people where they would expect to be in public view and not where they expect privacy or obviously look as if they are trying to keep their privacy. *This will sometimes come down to the subjective judgement of the researcher who may not always get it right. There are also special problems here of being unable to get informed consent or to debrief participants.*

The ninth guideline is concerned with giving advice. If the psychologist thinks they have discovered a problem that the participant does not know about, there is a moral obligation to let the participant know and to help them get further advice if they want to. *This could be difficult if the psychologist does not feel properly qualified and it may cause the participant unnecessary worry if it turns out to be a false alarm.* The tenth guideline is to do with monitoring a colleague's research so that psychologists look out for each other. They have a responsibility to say if they think a colleague is not obeying ethical guidelines. This protects both the researcher concerned and the psychological community.

> This is an accurate run-through of the current guidelines. It is easy to see where they could have been expanded or supported with illustrative examples, but the examiner must also bear in mind the strict time-limit the candidate is bound by.

Answer to part (b)

As with all guidelines, these are there to help psychologists but there are times when they will have to exercise their own judgement. Gross (1994) says 'every research situation is an ethical situation' but in some the ethical issues are more obvious than others. The two examples I am going to use are Milgram's obedience to authority study and Zimbardo's prison-simulation study.

> Good, this candidate is clearly on course and gets to the point straight away.

Milgram wanted to test the 'Germans are different' hypothesis. To do this he needed to obtain volunteers by deception and continue to deceive them to see how far they would go in obeying the authority of the researcher. The basic purpose of the investigation was to see how far people would go in administering what they thought were real electric shocks to another person while acting under orders from the researcher.

First, the advertisement Milgram placed said the study was on learning and memory which was not true. On arrival at the laboratory, participants were introduced to 'Mr Wallace' (not his real identity) and had to draw lots to see who would be the teacher and who the learner. The draw was fixed so the real participant was always the teacher. The electric shocks that the participant believed he gave Mr Wallace were non-existent. Mr Wallace had claimed he had a heart problem which he did not. *Milgram claimed that all this elaborate deception was necessary, otherwise he could not have gained valid results. As the participants were deceived, none could give informed consent so this particular guideline was also contravened.* During the study, some participants suffered severe psychological distress. *This led some critics, such as Baumrind, to complain that Milgram had not protected participants from harm.* Milgram also 'prodded' participants to go on when they said they wanted to stop *which goes against their right to withdraw whenever they wanted to.*

Milgram was attacked on ethical grounds but he defended himself and showed that he had followed ethical standards all along. He said he could not have tested his hypothesis without deception as he needed to make the authority convincing. He pointed out that all the participants could have disobeyed the experimenter and withdrawn if they had wanted to, although the fact that some participants were so obviously distressed should have led him to stop the proceedings immediately. Milgram's defence was that the distress was not sufficient to merit stopping but this is clearly a subjective judgement.

Milgram claimed he had taken the participants' right to protection into account but he had not expected them to go on administering shocks even when it appeared Mr Wallace was dead. He felt he had protected himself by showing his research design to other psychologists and students who had agreed it was acceptable. Milgram had an elaborate debriefing process ready after the research consisting of counselling, interviews and follow-up questionnaires. He claimed that all these showed the participants were not affected long-term by what they had been through. Some even thought it had done them some good. In fact, an impartial psychiatrist assessed the participants a year after the study and said there were no signs of psychological harm. In this way, Milgram fulfilled his responsibility to ensure that participants were restored, as far as possible, to their former state.

Milgram felt the means justified the ends in his research and that critics are more upset by the thought that anyone will obey an unknown authority than by the research procedures themselves. Although the American Psychological Association initially suspended Milgram, they eventually judged his work to be ethical and he was later awarded a prize for making an outstanding contribution to research.

> **A good attempt at assessment here. The candidate cannot avoid description in places but has still focused most of the material on Skill B. There is a good balance between identifying ethical issues and addressing them.**

Zimbardo carried out a research design that overcomes many of the objections to Milgram's but he still ran into problems. He set up a simulated prison in the basement of Stanford University and obtained young, adult male volunteers to be prisoners or guards. *Zimbardo did not deceive the participants at any time. He was completely honest with them and gained their informed consent. He could also be said to have taken their general welfare into account by hand-picking psychologically healthy young men with no criminal record and telling the 'guards' that they could not use physical means to control prisoners. They should have been well able to cope.*

As the prison study continued, the prisoners became more and more apathetic and distressed and the guards more brutal. The guards forced the prisoners to do demeaning things. One by one, prisoners were released because of the distress they were in. The study had been meant to last two weeks but Zimbardo stopped it after six days *which showed that he took the prisoners' distress to be implicit withdrawal and acted in their best interests.*

As with Milgram's study, it could be argued that the participants were not properly protected from harm. Some of them suffered disorganized thinking and depression which are risks not normally encountered in everyday life. Perhaps the right to withdraw was not made clear enough to the prisoners. Zimbardo stopped the study early but this might not have been soon enough. To defend himself, Zimbardo described all the debriefing procedures the participants went through such as counselling sessions with the researchers and guards and follow-up questionnaires and interviews. *Zimbardo agreed that participants (prisoners) had an unpleasant experience but he was sure it did not have long-term effects. Some of them even made use of it by giving interviews to American magazines and discussing it on their college courses. In the end the good effects of the study seem to outweigh the bad but it is still an issue whether the ends justified the means and whether anything really useful had been learned to justify what the participants went through.*

These studies show that no code of ethics can anticipate all possible problems in research. Psychologists sometimes have to adjust or stop their procedures as they go along if it appears that ethical standards are not being met.

The candidate has stuck closely to the question requirements here and resisted the temptation to give detailed accounts of the two studies and their findings.

Part (a) of this essay is straightforward, well-informed and well-structured. A little more detail would be necessary for full marks, hence 11 out of 12 (top of Band 3). Part (b) contains good material and addresses the 'attempts to overcome' part of the question quite well. The treatment of Milgram's study is very good and much more detailed than for Zimbardo. This slight imbalance makes 10 a likely mark for this part (top of Band 3), giving a total of 21 out of 24.

Solutions
Methodology, research design and statistics

SOLUTION TO REVISION ACTIVITIES

Revision activity 1   Psychological research methods

Table 21: Revision activity 1: Psychological research methods

Method	*Description*	*Example*	*Comments*
Observation.	*Watching and recording in order to arrive at a description of behaviour.*		*Problems of participant reactivity.* *Problems in choosing what to observe.* *Worthwhile at the start of new research for establishing the nature of something.*
Non-participant observation.	Observing from 'outside', taking a 'fly on the wall' approach. Can be		*Has the advantage of greater objectivity.*
	▶ *naturalistic, or*	Ethological studies e.g. of territoriality.	Less control but greater ecological validity.
	▶ *controlled.*	Ainsworth's 'strange situation' for measuring attachment type.	*More control but less ecological validity.*
Recording techniques include:			
▶ baby biography and diary description	Detailed written description of behaviour often in infants and children.	*Carried out by Darwin and Piaget respectively.*	Rich accounts but objectivity harder to achieve.
▶ specimen description	*A full account of a segment of the participants' life.*	'One Boy's Day', Barker and Wright (1951)	As above, and could be unrepresentative.
▶ event sampling	Recording incidences of a particular kind of behaviour, its context, antecedents and consequences.	Bell and Ainsworth (1972). Mothers'responses to infant crying.	*Time-saving; context preserved but reductionist.*
▶ time sampling.	Recording behaviour in specified, regular segments of time.	*Observations of playground aggression or play, say in one minute out of every five.*	*Quick and efficient but descriptions may be fragmented with context lost.*
Participation observation.	*Researcher becomes part of a group in order to study it from the 'inside'.*	Festinger et al. (1956) infiltrated 'The Seekers', a quasi-religious group who believed the world was about to end.	*Raises particular ethical problems.* Potentially rich and detailed understanding of group but danger of becoming a 'non-observing participant'.

(Continued)

Table 21 *Continued*

Method	Description	Example	Comments
Case Study	An in-depth study of a single instance of something. It can be a study of an individual but could also be of a couple, a famiily, a school, etc. It is an idiographic method aimed at gaining a detailed understanding of the individual case.	Many examples can be quoted, e.g. Allport's work on personality, Freud's psychoanalytic case studies, *Gregory and Wallace's study of SB's recovery from blindness, Ebbinghaus's study of his own memory.*	Uses a variety of data-collection methods, all with inherent strengths and weaknesses. *Detailed but could be narrow in focus. More open to subjective interpretation. May use unreliable retrospective accounts.* Not always readily generalizable but a number of similar case studies could be.
Surveys	Used for gathering data from large numbers of people using questionnaires and interviews Questionnaires can contain *open or closed questions* and be completed face-to-face, by post or by telephone. Interviews can be *structured, semi-structured or unstructured.*	Attitude surveys, e.g. Sears Maccoby and Levin (1957) on child-rearing styles; *The Hite Report* (1977) on female sexual behaviour; *Freud and Piaget developed clinical interviewing techniques.*	Difficulties with devising unambiguous questions that avoid bias, 'leading' the respondent or causing offence. *Respondents may answer to give a socially favour-able impression. (Guaranteeing anonymity might help avoid this.) Good sampling is vital if the results are to be of general use.*
Correlation	Not a research method in itself but a widely used statistical technique for detecting *linear relationships* in samples of paired data. Such analysis can be applied to data collected in a variety of ways. Correlation coefficients vary from *+1.00 to −1.00.*	Widely used in *concordance* studies e.g. genetic resemblance studies of IQ or the incidence of certain mental disorders. Can be used to show links between early experience and later behaviour, e.g. in media violence research or *in child-rearing patterns.*	*Correlation does not imply causation.* Useful for detecting patterns that may suggest new hypotheses for experimental testing. *Useful where experimental inter-vention would be unethical.*
Psychometric testing	The measurement of psychological attributes such as intelligence or personality using various testing techniques and usually yielding *quantitative* data.	IQ tests such as the *Stanford Binet or the Wechsler Scales* Personality tests such as the *Eysenck Personality Inventory or Cattell's 16PF.*	Tests must be reliable, valid and standardized. *Precise and objective.* Best used as part of overall assessment. *Interpretation of test results and access to test data raise important ethical issues.*
Content analysis	A way of making qualitative information quantitative, perhaps by setting up categories into which instances of events can be counted.	Used to examine content of media (e.g. Cumberbatch, 1990) *or of social discourse, or of verbal protocol in creating computer simulations.*	Helps to make qualitative data available for statistical analysis. *Open to accusations of reductionism. Useful in 'new paradigm' research.*
Experiment	Manipulation of IV in order to observe corresponding changes in DV while holding extraneous variables constant. Includes:	Many examples can be drawn from behavioural, cognitive, comparative and bio-psychology.	Enables us to identify *cause and effect.* Must be aware of confounding variables. Can be criticized for being dehumanizing.
	► *laboratory experiment*	► IV and research environment controlled	
	► field experiment	► *IV controlled but not research environment*	*Experimental control lessens as we move down this list but there is a corresponding gain in ecological validity.*
	► *quasi-experiment*	► IV occurs naturally, environment controlled	
	► natural experiment.	► *IV and environment naturally occurring.*	

Revision activity 2   Research methodology and statistics

These answers are meant to be illustrative but not exhaustive. You may find other equally valid ways of answering the questions which would be credited by an examiner.

Answers to general method questions

1 An experiment is an investigatory technique in which an IV is manipulated and the effects of this on a DV are observed and measured. Other (extraneous) variables are held constant. A true experiment is one in which the IV is directly under the experimenter's control (as in laboratory or field experiments). In natural and quasi-experiments the IV varies on its own and some would argue that, because of this, they are not really experiments.

2 The main difference between an experiment and a correlation is that experiments enable us to talk about 'cause and effect' whereas correlations simply describe patterns of linear relationship between pairs of data and do not allow us to make cause-and-effect statements. An experiment is also a research method but correlation is a technique of data analysis applied to data gathered by some other means.

3 An IV is the influence which a researcher manipulates in an experiment in order to observe its effect on a DV. In a study of the effect of alcohol on driving ability, the IV would be the amount of alcohol given to the drivers.

4 A DV is the factor in an experiment which is influenced by changes in the IV and which is observed and measured by the researcher. In the example given in (3), the DV would be driving ability.

5 A confounding variable is an influence in an experiment that is not the IV yet causes changes in the DV. For example, researchers may find age affects IQ in that older people do less well than younger people. However, this could be because of the confounding variable of how the test is approached. Older people may be more careful and less concerned about 'beating the clock' than younger people; consequently, their scores are lower.

6 Extraneous variables are all other variables apart from the IV and DV that need to be controlled in an experiment, such as the testing environment, time of day, instructions to participants. If extraneous variables are not taken care of they could obscure the effect of the IV or even turn into a confounding variable.

7 In a simple two-sample experiment, control-group participants are affected by everything the experimental group experiences with the exception of the IV. Scores form the control group, thus provide baseline data against which scores from the experimental group can be compared.

8 These are experimental designs used to control variation caused by individual differences between participants. In a simple experiment comparing two conditions, the independent group's design consists of two different groups of participants who have been allocated by chance to either of the two conditions. Matched pairs designs involve pairing participants on variables relevant to the study, then splitting the pairs and randomly allocating the members of the pair to one or other condition. In a repeated measures design, participants undergo both conditions in the experiment.

9 Practice effects occur in repeated measures designs when participants carry over an improvement to the second experimental condition as a result of having done the first condition. In this case, practice is a confounding variable.

10 Order effects occur in repeated measures designs when participants' performance in the second condition is affected by them having done the first. This could include improvements, as in practice effects, but it also includes the detrimental effects of fatigue or boredom.

11 Counterbalancing is built into repeated measures designs as a precaution against order or practice effects. Half the participants do condition A first, followed by B, and half do B first, followed by A, hence the term ABBA design.

12 Randomization has a number of meanings. It can refer to the random allocation of participants to conditions to help control for variation caused by the participants. Second, it can refer to randomizing the order in which participants take part in conditions (thus achieving a similar effect to counter-balancing). Third, it can refer to randomizing the order of stimulus materials for each participant, for example, a word list in a memory experiment might be given on a different order to each participant.

13 The mean number of words recalled under the imagery condition is higher than the mean number of words recalled under the repetition condition.

14 There is no difference in the mean number of words recalled under imagery and repetition conditions.

15 A directional hypothesis predicts the direction in which results will fall, for example, the mean of sample A is higher than the mean of sample B or the correlation between C and D is positive. Such hypotheses are used only when we have good reason to predict the direction of the results, for example, when previous research or careful reasoning suggest it.

16 A non-directional hypothesis does not predict the direction in which results will fall, for example, if the means of sample A and sample B differ or there is a correlation between C and D. Such hypotheses may be used when there is no prior reason to suppose that the results will turn out a particular way.

17 A one-tailed test is used with a directional hypothesis.

18 A two-tailed test is used with a non-directional hypothesis.

19 Operationalization means precisely defining a variable so that it can be measured. Aggression could be operationalized in many ways. One possibility would be to decide what constitutes verbal aggression and measure the number of incidences per hour. Alternatively, aggression could be measured as the number of incidences of physical violence per hour.

20 Demand characteristics are aspects of the research situation that could alert the participants to the hypothesis being tested. Participants may then alter their behaviour in accordance with the perceived demands of the situation.

21 Experimenter effects are influences (usually unwittingly) brought into the research situation by the experimenter, which can interfere with the study. They include the effects of the experimenter's appearance or behaviour on the participants but, most importantly, they include 'experimenter expectancy effects'. These occur when the experimenter somehow sways the results in the expected direction.

22 Participant reactivity refers to the possibility that participants' behaviour can be affecting the research situation so that they feel unable to react naturally. They may, for example, try to support or undermine the research. Alternatively they may be 'evaluatively apprehensive': concerned about making a favourable impression.

23 The single-blind procedure is when the participants are not informed of the research hypothesis. It is used when it is felt that their knowledge of the hypothesis would adversely affect the results or make a nonsense of the research procedure. It helps to minimize participant reactivity.

24 The double-blind procedure is when neither the participants nor the researcher gathering the data know the research hypothesis. The researcher is simply acting on instructions from another researcher. This is to minimize both experimenter effects and participant reactivity.

25 In one sense, a population is the total number of individuals that would qualify to take part in a research study because they have the necessary characteristics. In another sense, we can think of this as a population of potential data.

26 A sample is the group of individuals (or data) selected from a population for the purposes of a research study.

27 Sampling is carried out in order to ensure that the sample adequately *represents* the parent population so that findings from the sample can be *generalized* back to the population from which it was drawn.

28 In a random sample, each member of the population must have an equal chance of being selected. To achieve this, members of the population would be assigned a number and the required number of participants would be selected by picking out their numbers at random, either by using random number tables/generators or by pulling the numbers out of a hat.

29 The ideal sample size is that which adequately represents the parent population. A relatively larger sample would be needed to represent a very varied population and a relatively smaller one to represent a very homogenous population. For these reasons it is not sufficient to say an adequate sample size is, for example, 10% of the population.

30 Opportunity sampling is when the researcher takes the first people encountered who fit the necessary criteria. Quota sampling is like a more elaborate form of opportunity sampling and is often used by market researchers. They decide on a number of categories of individual that they'd like to study, how many to find from each category, and then go and opportunity sample them.

31 Another word for this is *consistency*. It usually means that a test or research study *can be depended upon* to produce the same, or similar, results every time it is carried out.

32 Inter-observer reliability is evident when different observers record the same event in the same way as each other. Test-re-test reliability is when a test produces similar results on two or more occasions. Alternate forms reliability is shown when two equivalent versions of the same test produce similar results.

33 Another word for validity is *relevance* or *appropriateness*. A clumsier way of putting it is to say that a measure is valid if it measures what it purports to measure.

34 Experimental validity refers to the internal 'worth' of the research design: is it really measuring what it is supposed to measure or are biases or other design problems getting in the way?

35 Findings from a research study have ecological validity if they have relevance in a real-life setting.

36 Face validity means that a measure appears, on the surface, to measure what it purports to measure. Predictive validity means that a measure is a good forecast of some future measure of performance. Content validity means that a test contains items that are appropriate for testing whatever it purports to test.

37 Standardization can refer to ensuring that conditions in a research setting are the same for all participants (perhaps with the exception of the IV). It is also used in the field of testing to refer to the process by which a test is adjusted until scores on it yield a normal distribution.

38 Standardized instructions are directions that are given to research participants in the same way. It is a form of control used in order to avoid favouring some participants over others.

39 A pilot study is a small-scale dummy-run of a proposed research procedure. Its purpose is to reveal any deficiencies in the procedure so that they can be put right, and the procedure perfected, before the full-scale study is carried out.

40 A cross-sectional research design involves selecting a number of different age groups of participants and studying them at the same time. A longitudinal research design usually means selecting one group of participants all within the same age range and following them up at intervals over time. Both research designs are aimed at discovering the nature of change with age.

Statistics questions
41

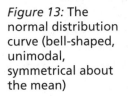

Figure 13: The normal distribution curve (bell-shaped, unimodal, symmetrical about the mean)

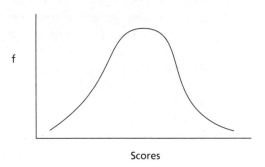

Scores

42

(a) a negatively skewed distribution

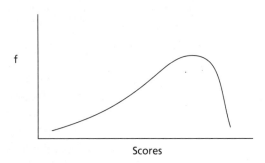

Scores

(b) a positively skewed distribution

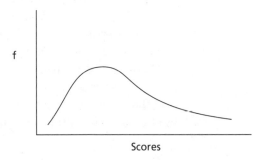

Scores

(c) a bimodal distribution

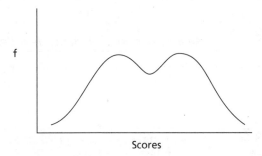

Scores

Figure 14: (a) A negatively skewed distribution (b) A positively skewed distribution (c) A bimodal distribution

43 Measures of central tendency are used for summarizing large amounts of data into one typical, or average, value.

44 The mean is the sum of scores divided by the number of scores. The median is the central score in a list of rank-ordered scores. The mode is the most frequently occurring value in a set of scores.

45 The median is preferred to the mean when the distribution of scores is skewed as a result of there being a small number of atypical scores (either high or low). The mean is easily distorted by such scores but the median is not affected by them.

46 Measures of dispersion are used to indicate the amount of variability, or spread, in a sample of scores.

47 The standard deviation, range and variation ratio are all measures of dispersion.

48 A z-score (or standard score) is the number of standard deviations a particular score is away from the sample mean.

49 The four levels of measurement are nominal, ordinal, interval and ratio.

50 Correlation can vary between $+1.00$ and -1.00.

51 The two correlation values are the same strength as each other because the numerical value (0.8) is the same. They differ only in that they show relationships in different directions: positive and negative.

52 Degrees of freedom.

53 The probability that something (usually a test result) occurred by chance is 5% or 5 in 100 or 1 in 20. The probability that something occurred by chance is 1% or 1 in 100. The probability that something occurred by chance is less than 5% or 5 in 100 or 1 in 20. The probability that something occurred by chance is less than or equal to 5% or 5 in 100 or 1 in 20. The probability that something occurred by chance is greater than 5% or 5 in 100 or 1 in 20. The probability that something occurred by chance is greater than 1% or 1 in 100.

54 The 0.05 level of significance is thought to strike a reasonable balance between the probability of making a Type I or Type II error in psychological research that is not of life-or-death importance.

55 A Type I error is an error of optimism resulting from rejecting the null hypothesis when it should be retained. Such an error can be made less likely by choosing a more stringent significance level.

56 A Type II error is an error of pessimism resulting from retaining the null hypothesis when it should be rejected. Such an error can be made less likely by choosing a less stringent significance level.

57

Table 22: Completed answer to question 57

| | Experiment | | Correlation | Association |
	Related design	Independent design	Correlation	Association
Data suitable for a parametric test	Related t test	Independent t test	Pearson's product moment correlation coefficient	
Data suitable for a non-parametric test	Wilcoxon test or sign test	Mann Whitney U test	Spearman's rho	Chi-square test

58 The three assumptions are: the data should be measured on an interval or ratio scale; the parent populations of data from which sample data are drawn should be normally distributed; the sample variances should be similar (there should be homogeneity of variance).

59 Parametric tests are sometimes said to be robust because they can withstand some violation of the underlying assumptions and still give a fairly accurate result.

60 The power of a test refers to its ability, relative to a non-parametric test, to detect a significant effect when the null hypothesis is false. Another way to put this is that it is the ability of the test to avoid making a Type II error.

QUESTIONS AND MARKED SAMPLE ANSWERS

Comments appear only for some answers and for those which did not earn full marks.

Question 4

(a) In a laboratory experiment, the researcher has control over the setting of the study. In the natural experiment this occurs naturally. In a laboratory experiment the researcher has control of the IV but in the natural experiment it occurs naturally. *(2 marks)*

(b) The experimenter does not have control over all the variables so will not be sure what causes changes in the DV.

Another reason needed here, such as problems with replication or with generalizing beyond the specific experimental situation. *(1 mark out of 2)*

(c) This is watching and recording behaviour in a natural environment. *(1 mark)*

(d) The researcher must consider the ethics of observing people and try to get their consent, only this might lead to participant reactivity. Also there is no control over the environment which could make it difficult to decide what is causing the behaviour. The researcher would have to decide how to record the behaviour and ensure the measure they use is valid.

The first sentence really covers two points. The second point and third points are relevant but could do with being expanded. *(just 3 marks)*

Question 5

(a) The researcher could take a random sample.

For 2 marks the choice of sampling technique must be both identified and explained. *(1 mark out of 2)*

(b) I would use an independent groups design and randomly allocate children to conditions. This way chance should even out any variables between groups. A matched pairs design probably wouldn't work because it would be difficult to know what to match children on. Repeated measures would not work because the children would probably be able to work out what the researcher's hypothesis was from doing one condition and then the other and this would make the results invalid. *(3 marks)*

(c) The most important thing would be inter-rater reliability. If four interviewers were being used they would all need to be trained to interview children in exactly the same way to avoid bias.

For 3 marks, go on to explain what is meant by inter-rater reliability, what sort of bias might occur and how reliability could be checked. *(2 marks out of 3)*

Question 6

(a) The median is a measure of central tendency found by ranking a set of scores and taking the middle score. *(1 mark)*

(b) The median is preferred when a set of data includes an extreme score which would distort a mean. It is also preferred with ordinal data. *(2 marks)*

(c) There is a strong positive correlation between the two sets of scores. High scores on one go with high scores on the other, but it can't be said that one causes the other. *(2 marks)*

(d) The Spearman's rho.

Good choice of test but no reason is given. The candidate could add that it is a test for linear relationships between paired scores. *(1 mark out of 3)*

Total 19 marks out of 24

part IV
Timed practice papers with answers

Question paper for Social and comparative psychology

Allow 45 minutes for *each* question.

Question 1
(a) Explain what is meant by the term 'conformity' *(4 marks)*
(b) Outline **two** studies of conformity *(8 marks)*
(c) Analyse studies of conformity in terms of what they can tell us about independent behaviour. *(12 marks)*

Question 2
Discuss **two** psychological research studies of obedience. *(24 marks)*

Question 3
Critically consider explanations of any **one** example of animal learning in the natural environment. *(24 marks)*

Question 4
Critically consider research into animal language. *(24 marks)*

OUTLINE ANSWERS

Question 1
(a) Explain what is meant by the term 'conformity'. *(4 marks)*
(b) Outline **two** studies of conformity. *(8 marks)*
(c) Analyse studies of conformity in terms of what they can tell us about independent behaviour. *(12 marks)*

> *Examiner's note:* Parts (a) and (b) of this question have Skill A injunctions, so in these you need to show knowledge and understanding. Clear explanations, good description and illustrative examples are called for. Notice that part (b) asks for outlines so do not be tempted to lapse into detailed evaluation. Your chance to show Skill B comes in part (c) where you are asked to apply your understanding of conformity to independent behaviour to try to explain why people do not conform. In this part you are not restricted to the studies you used for part (b).

▶ For part (a) it is worth using a quote e.g. Aronson (1992) says conformity is 'a change in a person's behaviour as a result of real or imagined pressure from a person or group of people'. To elaborate on this you could give Mann's (1969) classification which includes normative conformity (i.e. compliance and true conformity) informational conformity and ingratiational conformity. Very brief explanations of each term would be helpful.

▶ For part (b) choose with care. Asch carried out more than one study but this may not give you enough detail. A safer way might be to choose Asch's original line-judging task and variations on this by Crutchfield. Give succinct accounts of what was done and what was found.

▶ In part (c) a sentence saying what you understand by the term 'independent behaviour' would be a good start.

▶ In Asch's studies the majority of responses were non-conforming ones. Offer a number of possible reasons for these results:

  – Non-conformists could have been truly independent or anti-conformist. In the latter case, behaviour is still determined by the group but it does inflate the incidence of apparent independence.

  – Participants may have wanted to avoid deindividuation and maintain uniqueness and individuality even if this put their acceptance in the group at risk. In the Asch study, acceptance in the group was less critical than in the Crutchfield study where participants may have been anxious to create the right impression.

  – Participants may have wanted to maintain a sense of control over events. Burger (1987) measured participants' desire for personal control and found high scorers resisted conformity in rating the funniness of jokes.

▶ In Crutchfield's experiments, the rate of conformity was affected by the issue being judged. People may be more inclined to act independently when they are well-informed and more likely to conform when they feel unsure.

▶ Moscovici (1976) showed the power of a consistently dissenting minority to encourage independence in Asch-type studies. Thus the provision of non-conforming models is important.

▶ Participants in these studies may have been playing the role they thought the situation demanded. In real-life settings, independence may be far greater. Usually we can discuss dilemmas with other people and it is rare for us to be left with no choice but to express a dissenting view.

▶ The rate of independence could be affected by the level of moral reasoning.

▶ Cultural background and the timing of such studies may also play a part. Replications of Asch's study show that rates vary with culture and, since the 1950s, a greater tendency to act independently is evident in the USA and Britain (e.g. Nicholson *et al.*, 1985). Why do you think this is?

▶ Conclude with a consideration of how independence might be increased. Encouraging people to question the reasons why they are being asked to conform and informing them of the pressures which occur in such situations could help to fore-arm them and help them to remain independent.

Question 2

Discuss **two** psychological research studies of obedience. *(24 marks)*

> *Examiner's note:* A question like this would be very popular because it seems easy, so do be sure that you can do justice to Skills A and B. It is important both to describe (Skill A) and evaluate (Skill B) in equal depth.

▶ Say what you understand by obedience and identify which studies you will be using. Milgram's obedience to authority study and Zimbardo's prison-simulation study are good choices.

▶ Describe your two chosen studies as concisely as you can. You only have about ten minutes for each study, so think carefully about which details are really necessary. Detailed descriptions of the electric shock scales or guards' uniforms will have to go.

▶ Evaluate on practical grounds. Here you could examine the methodology of the studies and question their ecological validity.

▶ Evaluate on theoretical grounds, for example, the soundness of Milgram's agency theory; the emphasis on context and social roles in Zimbardo's work.

▶ Evaluate on ethical grounds. Both of these studies attracted criticism but both were eventually deemed to be within acceptable limits. The knowledge gained was thought to justify the means.

▶ Evaluate by reference to further studies, such as Hofling's (1966) study of obedience in nurses; attempts to replicate the study at other times and in other cultures.

▶ Have the studies shown us anything useful about obedience? Both studies have made important contributions to knowledge in potentially socially sensitive areas and raised people's awareness of issues relating to authority and obedience. Perhaps a better understanding of how people can collude in allowing authorities to exercise power (see Staub, 1990) and how they can resist obeying if they so wish will encourage more thoughtful independent action.

Question 3
Critically consider explanations of any **one** example of animal learning in the natural environment. *(24 marks)*

> *Examiner's note:* The injunction invites you to show knowledge and understanding of explanations of your chosen area of animal learning (Skill A) and an awareness of their strengths and limitations (Skill B). The AEB syllabus requires you to include foraging and homing in your study of this area but the question has not stipulated these so it is perfectly acceptable to choose something else if you feel that you are well-informed enough to do it justice. Do be sure to choose just one example. There will be no extra credit for providing more than one unless you can justify it.

▶ Foraging behaviour would be a good choice to use in your answer. Start by explaining what foraging is, why it is necessary and some of the many forms it can take, such as from parasitism to predation.
▶ Optimal Foraging Theory (OFT) takes a cost-benefit approach. Explain what this means.
▶ OFT also recognizes that foraging includes a wide range of behaviours apparently designed to optimize diet, reveal the profitability of search patch and search path. Illustrate each of these with an example.
▶ OFT has limitations in that some foraging does not appear to be optimal. Animals may sometimes sacrifice optimality in favour of protection of the young or territory defence or because they have to compete with others for food. Given the uncertainties of their world, they are more likely to have generally effective 'rules of thumb' for foraging rather than mathematically precise optimal rules. The model is therefore imperfect but not necessarily useless. Continued research in this area will help to refine OFT.
▶ The role of learning in OFT is not clearly defined except to say that foraging patterns could be innate, learned or both. Nevertheless, it is apparent that, in some species, it plays an important part.
▶ You could then go on to illustrate degrees of learning apparent in different species, such as the tendency of the toad to lie in wait and snap at small, dark, moving objects. This is in stark contrast to the flexible, and often cooperative, stalking behaviour of lionesses. Von Uexküll (1934) proposed that animals acquire a 'search image': they learn the stimulus characteristics of a particular food and this enables them to distinguish it more efficiently in the future. Some animals 'cache' or store food and have a phenomenal, if unexplained, capacity for relocating many stores.
▶ The principles of classical conditioning, operant conditioning and observational learning have all been observed in animals' foraging behaviour. Illustrate these with examples.
▶ The flexibility conferred by being able to learn appears to give a selective advantage to certain individuals and improve their fitness. They are more likely to survive and reproduce and to have young who inherit their parents' adaptive tendencies.

Question 4
Critically consider research into animal language. *(24 marks)*

Examiner's note: The injunction invites you to show knowledge and understanding of theories and/or studies of your chosen area of animal language (Skill A) and an awareness of their strengths and limitations (Skill B). The AEB syllabus gives natural animal language (e.g. in vervet monkeys or bees) or attempts to teach human language to non-human animals as *examples*. It does not specify which you should do, so either or both could legitimately be used to answer this question. You will need to decide whether to go for breadth or depth.

▶ Begin by indicating how you intend to answer the question. In the time you have, it might be sensible to treat one area in detail. Attempts to teach human language to primates would be a good choice.

▶ Outline the reasons for research in this area. For example, it is an interesting academic exercise; it addresses the question of continuity between species; it contributes to our understanding of animal cognition.

▶ Explain what human language is like. It could be seen as a sophisticated signalling system using words. Hockett's sixteen 'design features' are useful here but don't get involved in describing each in detail. Pick a few key features to illustrate what you mean.

▶ Dispense with early studies very briefly. Gardner and Gardner's study of Washoe can be given more time, especially in terms of whether Washoe showed evidence of the design features. Terrace's (1974) criticisms of these studies can be incorporated here, along with as many other methodological problems you can think of.

▶ Bring the essay up to date using research by Savage-Rumbaugh (1990 onwards) using the lexigram and more naturalistic teaching techniques. Some of the achievements of Kanzi could be brought in here.

▶ In spite of the remarkable achievements of Savage-Rumbaugh's chimps, the jury is still out on whether they really can acquire language. A human's use of language is flexible and sophisticated and it is questionable whether other animals can come anywhere near acquiring it when they are clearly not adapted for it.

▶ If you have time, mention studies which have used other species such as dolphins and parrots. An important contribution of such studies is that they emphasize language comprehension rather than production, leading some trainers (e.g. Pepperberg, 1990) to claim that language enhances animals' learning ability. This gives a useful added dimension to the whole area of animal language.

3,4 Question paper for
Bio-psychology and abnormal behaviour

Allow 45 minutes for *each* question.

Question 1
Describe and evaluate psychological research into any **two** human biological rhythms. *(24 marks)*

Question 2
Discuss the contribution of psychological research to our understanding of the phenomenon of hypnosis. *(24 marks)*

Question 3
Compare and contrast **two** current models of abnormality in terms of *either* their ethical *or* practical implications. *(24 marks)*

Question 4
(a) Describe any **one** system of classification used in the diagnosis of abnormal behaviour. *(12 marks)*
(b) From a psychological viewpoint, assess some of the problems involved in classifying abnormal behaviour. *(12 marks)*
(AEB Module 5 section B or terminal Paper 2 section D specimen question)

 OUTLINE ANSWERS

Question 1
Describe and evaluate psychological research into any **two** human biological rhythms. *(24 marks)*

> *Examiner's note:* The Skill A and B injunctions are very clear here and marks are equally weighted between them. You must show knowledge and understanding of research into your two chosen biological rhythms and be able to make an informed judgement about the value of this research. Choose your two rhythms with care to ensure that you have sufficient material to write about and make sure you stick to rhythms that occur in humans. The relevance of evidence from animal research must be made explicit.

▶ Identify your two chosen rhythms. A good choice here would be sleep cycles and the human female menstrual cycle.
▶ These are examples of ultradian and infradian rhythms respectively. Tell the examiner what these terms mean and explain what exogenous and endogenous zeitgebers are.
▶ Describe the nature of a typical sleep cycle beginning with the transition from waking to sleeping. Go on to describe the characteristics of each stage of sleep, including REM sleep. Build in as much theoretical and empirical evidence as you can.
▶ Describe the nature of the human female menstrual cycle including the role of different hormones at each stage.

▶ Take each cycle in turn and evaluate the usefulness of the knowledge gained about it:

  – Studies of sleep deprivation tell us something about the functions of sleep. Such knowledge can also be useful in managing situations where sleep is disrupted through shift or time-zone changes or in dealing with certain kinds of insomnia.

  – The external zeitgebers governing the menstrual cycle in women are not well understood. There is a link with the circadian temperature rhythm. Understanding this can help in both contraception and conception.

  – The debate about whether to include pre-menstrual dysphoric disorder (PMDD) in DSM is highly controversial and, as yet, not fully resolved. On the one hand its inclusion would pathologize and stereotype women (Where is the research on the effects on males of male hormones?). On the other hand it could deny help to those who need it if, indeed, the pre-menstrual phase of the cycle is a serious problem for some women.

  – It is worth noting that to take a rhythm in isolation from others could be seen as reductionist. Humans do, after all, have more than 100 circadian rhythms alone.

  – Ultimately, understanding the nature and function of our biological rhythms is something that we should be able to turn to our advantage.

Question 2

Discuss the contribution of psychological research to our understanding of the phenomenon of hypnosis. *(24 marks)*

> *Examiner's note:* Here you are being asked to both describe (Skill A) and evaluate (Skill B). The latter should be reasonably easy to provide as the concept of hypnosis is a controversial area. Remember that 'research' can include both theory construction and empirical data collection. Although this topic is in the bio-psychology section of your syllabus, physiological states unique to hypnosis are not well-substantiated.

▶ Begin by defining hypnosis and explain the hypnotic state. Outline the techniques hypnotists use and describe the physiological and psychological features of the hypnotic state.

▶ Describe theories of hypnosis, for example, state (neo-dissociation) and non-state (role-playing) theories.

▶ Psychological research has helped to identify the numbers of people who are susceptible to hypnosis, to develop hypnotizability measures, to identify some characteristics of more easily hypnotizable people and to develop self-hypnosis as a self-help technique. Explain and illustrate with examples as you go along.

▶ Psychological research has helped to inform us about what hypnosis can realistically achieve in terms of pain relief, post-hypnotic suggestion and hypermnesia. Expand as far as you can on each of these, giving research examples wherever possible.

▶ Tests of hypnosis have included investigating the 'hidden observer' and comparing simulated hypnosis with actual hypnosis. There does appear to be some support for the validity of hypnosis but wide individual differences and problems with 'faking' and placebo effects mean that it remains a controversial concept.

Question 3

Compare and contrast **two** current models of abnormality in terms of *either* their ethical *or* practical implications. *(24 marks)*

> *Examiner's note:* Notice the choice available in this essay. In the heat of an

examination you could miss this and be tempted to write on more than two models. Students find 'compare and contrast' injunctions off-putting but careful organization can help a great deal. For Skill A you will need to show knowledge and understanding of the two chosen models. For Skill B you will need to identify similarities and differences and attempt to make an evaluation on the strength of these and the models themselves. Think carefully about your choice of models and whether it is better to go for practical or ethical considerations.

For information on models see Chapter 7 and the revision activity for Chapter 4.

For your two models compare and contrast the following:

► How behaviour is determined (environmentally, biologically or both).
► Basic assumptions about the origins of abnormality and what the symptoms represent.
► How they would explain the same condition(s).

If you choose to debate practical matters you could include:

► Treatments. The focus of these could be compared in terms of what assumptions they are based on, what form they take, what they aim to achieve and what they see as 'cure'.
► Openness to testability of underlying assumptions and therefore validation of the approach.
► Effectiveness for different conditions/breadth of application.
► Flexibility in terms of whether they apply general principles or can be fitted to the individual.
► Use of classification systems including nomothetic versus idiographic issues.
► Explanatory power, for example, of the 'neurotic paradox' and 'symptom substitution'.
► Where does responsibility for the condition lie? With the individual or the environment?
► The nature of the therapeutic relationship.

If you choose ethical issues you could adapt some of the practical points already mentioned as well as points in *Ethical issues in applying models of mental disorder* on pages 28–29.

Question 4
(a) Describe any **one** system of classification used in the diagnosis of abnormal behaviour. *(12 marks)*
(b) From a psychological viewpoint, assess some of the problems involved in classifying abnormal behaviour. *(12 marks)*
(AEB Module 5 section B or terminal Paper 2 section D specimen question)

Examiner's note: Two mini-essays are needed here with Skill A in part (a) and Skill B in part (b). Notice the requirement talk about just *one* system in part (a). The best documented classification system is DSM IV and this would be a good choice here. Notice also that part (b) is *not* restricted to just one approach.

Part (a)
Expand on these points as far as time allows.
► DSM IV is a widely used, American-based diagnostic and classification system listing about 300 mental disorders and their *essential* and *associated* features.
► The system also gives information relating to age, gender and culture in terms of the prevalence of disorders and risk, likely course, complications, predisposing factors and family patterns.

▶ The system is multi-axial, meaning that there are a number of variables on which a person can be assessed. Axis I lists clinical syndromes and Axis II classifies personality disorders and mental retardation. Symptoms are described in terms of their nature, onset, frequency, severity, duration and how they cluster together.

▶ Axis III covers general medical information, Axis IV takes environmental and psychosocial factors into account and Axis V makes a global assessment of functioning (GAF) focusing on the previous twelve months.

▶ Axes I and II provide a label. The other Axes add to this by helping with the overall management of a case.

Part (b)

Both practical and ethical problems should be addressed here. A summary of ideas can be found in *Classifying abnormality* on pages 26–27. In addition:

▶ Classification systems derive from the medical model with which not all practitioners would agree. Nevertheless they find classification helpful for research purposes and for communicating with each other, for example, when justifying particular courses of action in courts of law or in education.

▶ Such systems give an illusion of explanation but they are almost entirely descriptive.

▶ No system is foolproof but benefits must outweigh the costs.

▶ What can be done about the problems? Jettison the system? Work to improve it? Deliberately leave some categories 'fuzzy' rather than apply a rigid label?

▶ What are the alternatives? There is some support for a system based on descriptions of behavioural context and patterns. Still others prefer a psychodynamic approach.

5,6 Question paper for **Cognitive and developmental psychology**

Allow 45 minutes for *each* question.

Question 1
Critically consider **two** theories of memory. *(24 marks)*

Question 2
Describe and evaluate **two** explanations of forgetting. *(24 marks)*

Question 3
Critically consider the view that the self develops as a result of socialization. *(24 marks)*

Question 4
Compare and contrast **two** cognitive developmental theories of moral development. *(24 marks)*

OUTLINE ANSWERS

Question 1
Critically consider **two** theories of memory. *(24 marks)*

> *Examiner's note:* For the Skill A part of this question you need to show knowledge and understanding of your chosen theories and for Skill B, an awareness of their strengths and limitations. There is no explicit need to compare the theories or link them in any way but remember that the strengths of one are often the limitations of another. Allocate your time in four parts, two for descriptions and two for evaluation.

▶ State which two theories you have chosen. A good contrast is provided by 'boxology' approaches such as that of Atkinson and Shriffrin (1968) and Bartlett's constructivist approach.

▶ Outline the main characteristics of the memory stores in the two-process model, providing brief accounts of supportive evidence wherever possible (Skill A). You could slip in some Skill B here by commenting critically on the supportive evidence, for example, in terms of ecological validity.

▶ Offer general criticisms of the model itself, for example, its simplicity, the questionable role of rehearsal.

▶ Developments from the theory offer the most mileage for evaluation. Mention Baddeley, Paivio, Cohen and Squire. If you can fit in Wickelgren's (1974) single store model and Tulving's (1972) idea about episodic and semantic memory, so much the better.

▶ Describe your second theory. In this case, the idea of fitting material into existing schemata, even if this involves distortions, seems to explain the form memories take.

▶ An important feature of Bartlett's approach is his insistence on using more ecologically valid materials. The problems this presents for measurement could also be seen as a weakness.

▶ Bartlett's theory has been helpful in accounting for memory in everyday situations, for example, in EWT.

▶ The growth of the cognitive approach to memory is one important offshoot of this approach.

▶ Both models are useful in helping us to explain and reduce forgetting.

▶ Outline an alternative such as Craik and Lockhart's (1972) levels of processing model.

Question 2

Describe and evaluate **two** explanations of forgetting. *(24 marks)*

> *Examiner's note:* If you have revised models of memory well you should be in a good position to understand many explanations of forgetting but here you must focus on two. You could use other models to evaluate your chosen explanations but you must make this explicit, otherwise your essay will look like a general account of forgetting.

▶ Begin by identifying which two explanations you will focus on. Atkinson and Shiffrin's two-process model and Bartlett's constructivist approach have plenty to offer.

▶ Explain that 'forgetting' is quite a broad term and that it can result from breakdown at either the encoding, storage or retrieval stage. Offer a brief explanation of these terms, for example, that there are a number of different types of retrieval such as recognition, recall and redintegration.

▶ Explain forgetting from SIS, STM and LTM in the two-process model, remembering that the encoding, storage and retrieval characteristics of these stores all play a part. Loss of information from SIS is due to trace decay. From STM memory loss is due to either interference or decay. LTM information could be lost due to lack of retrieval cues, poor encoding or organization, physiological decay of the memory trace, or lack of context cues such as appropriate physical state.

▶ In Bartlett's view, forgetting is mainly to do with distorting material so that it is no longer exactly like the original. The distortions can be remembered by the mnemonic ORACA (see Topic Outline in Chapter 5).

▶ To evaluate, note how these models can help us to prevent forgetting, for example, by rehearsal, organization, cues for memory, avoidance of errors resulting from 'effort after meaning'.

▶ Also comment on the validity of the theories which underpin explanations of forgetting.

▶ Another way to evaluate is to comment on the alternatives which may fill in some of the gaps in your two chosen explanations. Good contrasts to the cognitive approaches used so far are psychodynamic ideas about motivated forgetting and behaviourist ideas about interference. An alternative cognitive view is Craik and Lockhart's (1972) levels of processing approach.

Question 3

Critically consider the view that the self develops as a result of socialization. *(24 marks)*

> *Examiner's note:* The injunction in this question requires you to show knowledge and understanding of socialization processes in the development of self (Skill A) and to show your awareness of the strengths and limitations of these explanations (Skill B). With a topic such as this, most of your Skill B commentary will be provided through presenting alternative viewpoints and evidence to support theory.

▶ It is quite a good idea to open with a few very short comments on 'self'. Theorists agree that a sense of self is not present at first but develops with time. It is the process by which this happens that is to be debated here.

▶ The view that self is a product of socialization is expressed in G. H. Mead's symbolic interactionism. In essence, he says that there is no sense of self at birth but it develops and changes through social interactions with others.

▶ Mead distinguished two parts of the self: the 'I' is the basic sense of self-awareness which is actively but not consciously experienced. It is free of influence from the views of others. The 'Me' is the sense of self as an object to others. It is passively received, socially influenced and includes such things as a sense of physical attributes, possessions, values, manner of thinking, reputation, roles and behaviour.

▶ Mead described the self as reflective in nature: we can reflect on ourselves in the same way that we reflect on others. Cooley (1902) had referred to this as 'the looking-glass self '.

▶ In order to reflect on ourselves, we need to learn to 'role-take': put ourselves in another's shoes and see ourselves as they see us. This initially happens in three stages defined by 'interactional age' rather than actual age.

▶ The stages are the preparatory stage, the play stage and the game stage. These should be briefly explained at this point. They are known collectively as 'primary socialization'.

▶ 'Secondary socialization' happens in adolescence and adulthood. Mead and his followers suggested a number of ways in which we gain information about our self, through feedback from significant others, comparison with others and roles played. Offer as much evidence and commentary as you can.

▶ Adolescents' 'body image' can be an important influence on self-concept as can maturation rate and birth order.

▶ Briefly offer some alternative views by way of evaluation, for example, psychodynamic and cognitive developmental theories.

Question 4

Compare and contrast **two** cognitive developmental theories of moral development. *(24 marks)*

> *Examiner's note:* For this question you need to point out the similarities and differences between your two chosen theories, such as Piaget, Kohlberg and Gilligan, although Eisenberg's model of pro-social reasoning is also useful. You could describe the two theories separately and then compare and contrast at the end or do it as you go along.

▶ Outline what you understand by the term 'cognitive developmental'. Immediately this is something the theories you will choose have in common. Name your chosen theories.

▶ Briefly describe the first theory, for example, Piaget's along with as much evidence and commentary as you can provide.

▶ Briefly describe your second theory, for example, Kohlberg's, again with commentary.

▶ Identify similarities, such as they are both stage theories, the stage sequence is seen as invariant, they both involve qualitative data-collection methods, both could be accused of Eurocentric bias.

▶ Identify differences: Piaget sees development as largely being completed in childhood and adolescence. Kohlberg took a lifespan view and accepted that not everyone would complete the stage sequence. Their chosen methods differed: Piaget studied children, Kohlberg chose a wider age range.

▶ Specific weaknesses of each theory are also a means of providing contrast. In Piaget's case, research has questioned whether everyone completes the stage sequence and raised doubts about his methods. Kohlberg has been criticized for his limited subject base (all male). Gilligan says this leads to androcentric bias and male morality, based on justice, being seen as superior. Women tend to use an 'ethic of caring' which scores lower on Kohlberg's scale.

▶ The conclusion could focus on the fact that both theories deal well with judgements of right and wrong but neither gives a complete explanation of morality: neither theory covers 'prosocial reasoning' (Eisenberg, 1986). Also, neither theory addresses moral feelings or the inconsistency between the level of reasoning and behaviour. Psychodynamic theory and social learning theory respectively are more successful at explaining these.

Question paper for
Perspectives, ethics, methodology and research design and statistics

Allow 45 minutes for *each* question.
Research Methods and Data Analysis (Specimen Question 2, Module Test PS2, for new NEAB, 1997 syllabus)

Question 1
A psychologist predicts, on the basis of previous research, that people with low self-esteem avoid situations where the focus of attention is on themselves.
A random sample of 72 people was obtained, and each person was given a standardized test that measured self-esteem. The psychologist used the scores from this test to assign people either high, medium or low self-esteem categories. Each person was then placed in a situation in which a choice had to be made between performing a task in front of other people ('audience' condition) or alone ('no audience' condition). The following data were obtained.

Table 23: Number of people choosing to perform in front of others (audience) or alone (no audience)

	Audience	No Audience
Low self-esteem	5	15
Medium self-esteem	14	14
High self-esteem	18	6

(a) What type of measurement scale do the above data represent? (*1 mark*)
(b) A Chi-square test was performed on the data shown in Table 23.
   (i) How many degrees of freedom are associated with these data and how is this determined? (*3 marks*)
   (ii) State the null hypothesis for this experiment. (*2 marks*)
   (iii) State *one* assumption to be met before a Chi-square could be used. (*2 marks*)
(c) The Chi-square value was significant: in view of this, interpret the data in Table 23. (*4 marks*)

The twenty people classified as low in self-esteem were offered a short therapy programme to help raise their self-esteem. Twelve took the programme and completed the same self-esteem test one month after the programme had been completed. Each person's score, after treatment, was compared with their original score, and coded as the same (i.e. no change), or increased or decreased self-esteem. Eight people showed an increase, one a decrease and three no change in self-esteem.

(d) Name two variables you would wish to control for in the second study. Briefly justify your answer. (*4 marks*)
(e) What test should be used to establish whether the therapy programme has been successful? Briefly justify your answer. (*3 marks*)
(f) Briefly discuss *one* ethical problem raised by this study. (*3 marks*)
(g) Design a further study to see whether the therapy programme remained

effective six months later. In this study you must devise a behavioural measure of self-esteem and not use a self-report measure. *(8 marks)*

Total: *30 marks*

Essay question 2
Discuss the reductionism debate as it applies to psychology. *(24 marks)*

Essay question 3
Critically consider some of the ethical issues raised by socially sensitive research in psychology. *(24 marks)*

OUTLINE ANSWERS

Question 1

Examiner's note: At the risk of stating the obvious, read the questions carefully, then look at the number of marks available for each part before answering. Be sure to do everything the examiner asks. For example, question (c) offers 4 marks for interpreting Table 23. Three of these are available for describing the results for each level of self-esteem and 1 for commenting on what this might mean. In question (d) there are 2 marks for identifying 2 variables and 2 marks for justifying your choice.

(a) The measurement scale is nominal.

(b) (i) There are 2 degrees of freedom because there are 3 rows and 2 columns of data.
Degrees of freedom = rows – 1 × columns – 1 (i.e. $2 \times 1 = 2$)

   (ii) There is no association between level of self-esteem and whether or not people choose to perform in front of an audience.

   (iii) The data must be independent i.e. a score must not appear in more than one cell. Or the expected frequencies should be 5 or more in 80% or more of the cells.

(c) Three times more low self-esteem participants chose to perform alone than in front of an audience. Medium self-esteem participants divided equally between the two conditions. Three times more high self-esteem participants chose to perform in front of an audience, than alone. This suggests that self-esteem is associated with choice of whether to perform alone or in front of an audience with higher self-esteem participants preferring an audience, lower self-esteem participants preferring no audience and medium self-esteem participants falling between the two.

(d) In the second study, participants would probably know the purpose of the self-esteem test and this might affect the way they answered. It would be better to disguise the purpose of the test if possible or build in a 'lie scale' to help check the validity of results. Another problem might be that participants differed in their previous experience of therapy. This might lead to them having differing expectations of success at the outset which would ultimately affect the results. Ideally they would all have the same amount of experience or none at all.
Note: There are many possible answers to this question. There is one mark for each variable and one further mark each for expanding on the problems they pose.

(e) Participants would score either + (increased self-esteem), – (decreased self-esteem) or 0 (no change). These scores are nominal and, as the researcher is testing for differences between two sets of related scores (before and after therapy), a sign test would be appropriate.

(f) It is important that the researcher protects the psychological wellbeing of participants and those with low self-esteem will be particularly vulnerable. The researcher should be prepared to spend time with all participants after the study to ensure that they leave the situation no worse than when they entered it. If the therapy does not work, or participants score lower than before, counselling must be made available for them if they wish to take it. (*Note:* Identify one problem for one mark and discuss its possible effects and/or how to deal with it for a further two marks.)

(g) To test the long-term effectiveness of the therapy programme, it would be necessary to devise a measure of self-esteem that could be used on the 'improvers' immediately after therapy and again six months later. The researcher might choose a variable known to correlate positively with self-esteem scores, for example, amount of eye-contact. The task might be to ask participants to memorize and recite a passage of prose to an audience. The participant's behaviour in terms of number of seconds eye-contact with the audience over a fixed time period could be discretely measured. All this would be repeated six months later using a matched prose passage and a similar audience so that scores from the two occasions could be compared. If self-esteem as measured by eye-contact remains unchanged, there should be no difference in the duration of eye-contact at the beginning and end of the six months. Increases or decreases in the amount of eye-contact could be taken to indicate changes in self-esteem for better or worse. (*Note:* Elaborate on potential confounding variables in this design and ethical issues if time allows.)

Question 2

Discuss the reductionism debate as it applies to psychology. *(24 marks)*

> *Examiner's note:* 'Discuss' requires you to show your understanding of the term 'reductionism' (Skill A) and to evaluate it in terms of its worth or appropriateness in psychology (Skill B).

▶ Offer some definitions of the term 'reductionism', for example, the idea that it is possible adequately to account for complex behaviour by breaking it down into smaller units which work together. The ultimate reductionism would be to explain behaviour at the level of micro-physics but any attempt to reduce complex behaviour qualifies as reductionism.

▶ Describe some types of reductionism, such as neurophysiological, biological, experimental and machine reductionism. Give examples (Skill A) and a strength and weakness (Skill B) for each.

▶ Evaluate by offering some views on reductionism. Putnam (1973) says: 'Psychology is as under-determined by biology as it is by elementary particle physics … people's psychology is partly a reflection of deeply held societal beliefs.' Legge (1975) uses the example of signing one's name to show how one action can be explained on many levels. Cohen (1977) argues that one level of explanation is sometimes enough (e.g. forgetting = decay in memory traces) but not always (e.g. addiction has a physiological level but its expression also depends on psychological and social factors). However, Rose (1976) says that to use one level to explain another is a fruitless exercise.

▶ Continue evaluating by offering alternatives, for example, autonomism, the 'slice of life' school and interactionism. Give examples and evaluative comments as you go along.

▶ Try to arrive at a balanced conclusion by saying what reductionism can and cannot offer psychology. If psychologists could agree on an appropriate and parsimonious level of explanation instead of having separate 'islands' of research it would unite them as scientists under one paradigm. Paradoxically, this could cause psychology to disappear. Many psychologists agree there will always be a need for different and multi-level explanations of behaviour; thus reductionism should enhance, not obliterate psychology.

Question 3

Critically consider some of the ethical issues raised by socially sensitive research in psychology. *(24 marks)*

> *Examiner's note:* The injunction 'critically consider' requires you to show knowledge and understanding of ethical issues in the stipulated area (Skill A) and to show an awareness of the strengths and limitations of the ideas presented (Skill B).

▶ Explain your understanding of the term 'socially sensitive'. For example, Sieber and Stanley (1988) say it includes 'studies in which there are potential social consequences or implications either directly for the participants in research or the class of individuals represented by the research'. Elaborate on this to show you understand its meaning: that such research could lead to short-term problems for the participants or wider consequences in terms of discrimination or 'social control'.

▶ Debate the definition of 'socially sensitive'. For example, Gross (1992) says 'we should regard *every* psychology experiment as an ethical situation' but are they all socially sensitive?

▶ Sieber and Stanley say psychologists should be aware of social sensitivity in at least four areas: the formulation of the research question, the conduct of research, the institutional context of research and the way results are interpreted. Try to illustrate each of these with examples.

▶ Offer some examples of socially sensitive research and talk through their possible consequences, for example, studies by Milgram and Zimbardo *et al.,* Sigmund Freud, Margaret Mead, Bowlby, Burt: any study which seeks a genetic basis for behaviour.

▶ Outline some of the risks to psychologists in socially sensitive research, for example, their findings may be distorted for political ends or rejected because people do not want to accept the findings.

▶ Consider psychologists' responsibilities. There are no formal ethical guidelines in such research but this does not mean it should be avoided. Scarr (1988) and Aronson (1992) agree that it must be done but that the public should be kept informed and empowered to prevent possible abuses of research findings. However, Howitt (1991) thinks that psychologists are not yet in a powerful enough position to alter social policy through their research but that they should be ready for a change to this situation.

LONGMAN
EXAM
PRACTICE
KITS

REVISION PLANNER

Getting Started — *Begin on week 12*

Use a calendar to put dates onto your planner and write in the dates of your exams. Fill in your targets for each day. Be realistic when setting the targets, and try your best to stick to them. If you miss a revision period, remember to re-schedule it for another time.

Get Familiar — *Weeks 12 and 11*

Identify the topics on your syllabuses. Get to know the format of the papers – time, number of questions, types of questions. Start reading through your class notes, coursework, etc.

Get Serious — *Week 10*

Complete reading through your notes – you should now have an overview of the whole syllabus. Choose 12 topics to study in greater depth for each subject. Allocate two topic areas for each subject for each of the next 6 weeks

No. of weeks before the exams	Date: Week commencing	MONDAY	TUESDAY
12			
11			
10			

There are lots of ways to revise. It is important to find what works best for you. Here are some suggestions:

- try testing with a friend: testing each other can be fun!
- label or highlight sections of text and make a checklist of these items.
- learn to write summaries – these will be useful for revision later.
- try reading out loud to yourself.
- don't overdo it – the most effective continuous revision session is probably between forty and sixty minutes long.
- practise answering past exam papers and test yourself using the same amount of time as you will have on the actual day – this will help to make the exam itself less daunting.
- pace yourself, taking it step by step.

WEDNESDAY	THURSDAY	FRIDAY	SATURDAY	SUNDAY

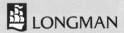